ENLIGHTENMENTS

FRANCISCO GALLARDO

G.F

Copyright ©2021 by Francisco Gallardo

Published by Francisco Gallardo

Book format: Francisco Gallardo

Cover Illustration: Francisco Gallardo

Graphic Design: Ricardo Ramirez

This book is about the lessons I have learned through my own experiences that can help you. However, I'm not certified to give professional advice to anybody about anything.

Although this is my reality, the names in this book have been fictionalized to avoid a dispute of any kind and prevent possible embarrassment.

ISBN 979-8-9853617-1-1 (pbk)

Second Edition

Dedication

This book is dedicated to my Mother, Silvia Gallardo, and my Father, Francisco Gallardo, for doing an exceptional job as parents.

This book is also dedicated to those trying to become better human beings and who refuse to let their circumstances define their success.

Lastly, this book is dedicated to my creator. This is my greatest effort yet, in faith to contribute to a better humanity.

Contents

Enlightenments part two

You're entitled to be subjective about things in your life, but it's better to be objective when you're trying to learn something new

71

Commandments:

I am the Lord your God: You should not have any strange Gods before me

78

You should not make idols

79

You should not take the name of your lord your God in vein

80

Remember to keep holy the Lord's Day

81

Honor your father and your mother

82

You should not commit adultery

83

You should not steal

87

You should not bear false witness

88

You should not covet

91

Introduction

Nature versus nurture is a concept in psychology that has a history of trying to understand whether human characteristics are influenced by heredity or learning and experiences.

When it pertains to this concept, nature refers to the influence genetics have on our characteristics, and nurture refers to our environment's influence on our characteristics.

Certain human characteristics are clearly influenced by nature. For instance, my genetics (nature) are the reason I was born with ten toes, two legs, ten fingers, two arms, two brown eyes, brown skin, and black hair. If I wanted to grow a different hair color, I just simply couldn't because it is not in my genetics (nature) to be able to do that. I could, however, dye my hair a different color, but that would be the influence of the environment (nurture) as opposed to genetics (nature).

Just like with nature, there are certain human characteristics clearly influenced by nurture. For instance, I learned to speak Spanish and English because of my environment (nurture). I was not born with the ability to speak Spanish or English because of my genes (nature). Language was taught to me by my environment (nurture).

Although physical human traits and language are great examples to use in distinguishing the idea of nature versus nurture, when it comes to MOST of our other characteristics, the source of influence is not as clear. While, throughout history, some psychologists believed most of our development was solely influenced by our genes, others believed most of our development was solely influenced by our environment. Now, researchers understand that both nature and nurture affect changes throughout life for almost all of our characteristics; it is not just one or the other.

A person's weight can be a good case in how the majority of our characteristics are influenced by both our genes and our environment. While weight can be influenced by how much and what somebody decides to eat (nurture), it can also be influenced by how somebody's anatomy digests how much and what they decide to eat (nature).

The motive behind starting my intro with the explanation of this theory is because I believe anybody who understands this concept (even if just subconsciously) has better odds of being successful. I will give you three reasons as parts of this intro explaining that logic.

Reason 1

If you don't acknowledge there are others born with better innate abilities than you, you will be disoriented about the amount of work required for you to be better than the competition.

When I was fourteen, I began practicing boxing and did so for about four years at a gym in a park called Scottsdale, located on the south side of Chicago. Most people I would spar with at that gym, in my weight division, were not a challenge to me. There was only one guy who was better than me. I had been told this guy did boxing since he was a child, and I would see him at the gym Monday-Friday, with his father constantly pushing him to improve.

The first time I sparred against him was about a year and a half after joining the gym.

It was an exciting session—we were both going at it intensely, exchanging about the same number of punches. By the end of the first round, we had a little crowd watching us. Close to the end of the final round, I became exhausted. Despite the fatigue, I kept up a good fight until he put me on my knees with an unexpected uppercut to the body in the last seconds of the fight.

His condition was superior to mine. While he knew precisely where and when to release punches to my body, I was not even considering that he could knock me down with a body shot.

While it was clear that this guy was better than me, one might wonder if he was born with better skills to box (nature), and the answer is no, based on the concept I just explained. If he was born with better skills to box, he would have dominated that fight from the start, and every other time we got in the ring, based on the experience and hard work he had over me (nurture). However, even with less training than him, I became almost as good at boxing in no time because the skills necessary to be good came naturally to me (nature). After our first fight, he was never able to suffocate me again or dominate any round clearly when we fought.

Nevertheless, this guy is an excellent depiction of somebody who understood he must work excessively to be able to compete with guys like me, and if he didn't, he would have been in trouble every time we got in that ring.

It is a fact that your genes can put you at an advantage or disadvantage when it comes to abilities you possess from birth. Therefore, it is your job to understand what you are innately good at and what you are not. If you are passionate about something you aren't naturally good at, you can still develop that passion into something great. However, you must understand it will require hard work on your part, especially if you're passionate about doing things that demand a high level of competition, like boxing. If you ignore this truth, you will constantly set yourself up for failure because your expectations will rarely meet your reality.

Reason 2

If you are born with innate abilities but disregard the importance of hard work, you might miss out on being great.

Michael Jordan, Tom Brady, Floyd Mayweather, and other athletes who were clearly better than their competition are examples of people with exceptional innate abilities nurtured to their full potential.

I believe there are and will be more people in this world who are born with just as much talent as these guys. Still, many will never recognize or take advantage of the superiority they were genetically born with (nature) because thorough understanding and development of anything is incredibly difficult (nurture).

Reason 3

TRUE HAPPINESS WILL COME FROM NURTURE OF THE MIND!

This reason is the most important in my opinion, and it's also why I decided to write this.

I recognized my ability to box early on, but I never worked hard enough to take it to another level because I simply never cared about boxing like that. However, I have worked very hard for other things that actually matter to me, like my well-being.

Being happy is a state of mind, and although perusing things you like such as sports, careers, hobbies etc., can add to your happiness, it won't be enough if you don't make the decision to develop your brain along with it.

This book is an autobiography filled with lessons that can most certainly help make your life better by influencing your mentality. And who knows, maybe you were born smarter than me and could do more with the following knowledge than I ever could.

So, are you ready to be enlightened?

It might seem arrogant to write an autobiography titled "Enlightenments" while not considered a famous person or a very "successful" one, but I am a successful person, and you can be too.

Success is subjective. You can't be a winner if you feel like a loser.

I consider myself successful for various reasons, and hopefully, you will enjoy my writing as much as I have.

†

Enlightenments part one

Focus on where you're at and where you want to be, not where you're from

I am a five feet eight inches, brown Mexican. I have lived most of my life in the south side of Chicago.

Chicago is a beautiful city, and it can be a good place to live in, but it has a lot of areas, especially on its south side — involved with a high rate of violence and poverty.

Living in an environment where prosperity isn't often visible can cause many people to feel like they should settle for a mediocre way of living, but that's the wrong mentality to adopt.

The environment you grow up around should never stop you from obtaining more than what is presented to you.

Whether you live in the Southside of Chicago or not, if you are a person living under shitty circumstances, you have to understand you are still in control of your life.

Stop focusing on where you're from and focus on where you are at and where you want to be. If you are not in a good place, work on how you can get there. Just because your environment offers a fucked up way of living does not mean you have to take it or you can't work to provide yourself with a better one.

In this life, your mentality will determine your success, not your circumstances.

Don't focus on insignificant shit

Here are some things I tell myself often to keep focus on what matters most:

I. As long as somebody isn't disrespecting you, do not focus on how a message is delivered; ask yourself if the message makes any sense.

II. Do not focus on who delivers the message; ask yourself if the message is any good.

III. Do not focus on whether strangers believe you're a good person or not, as long as the people you interact with daily know that you are.

IV. Do not focus on whether others believe you're capable of success or not; what matters most is if you believe that.

SIDE NOTE: The following stories are experiences that helped me grasp the messages I'm sharing, but the messages can apply to different scenarios. That is why certain messages will be repeated throughout my writing. Also, repetition is a good way to learn.

Take advice with a grain of salt, including advice from people with good intentions

I've always had friends growing up, but my first real close friend was Tip. I met Tip freshman year of High School. He was a six-foot, one-inch Mexican (yes, ladies, they exist) with light brown eyes and nice eyebrows.

Out of the eight class periods I had, Tip and I were together in seven. We were also both on the school's soccer team, which meant we spent a lot of time together. In just a matter of time, Tip and I became the best of friends.

During our sophomore year, I remember we got invited to one of our female friend's volleyball game.

At the game, I saw this junior that was very pretty to me, so I tapped him and said discreetly, "Ey bro! You see number ten? She cute as fuck! Ima try to get with her for sure."

Tip replied to me, saying, "You know I'm your boy, so I'm not trying to be a hater, but she's out of your league. I don't want you setting yourself up for disappointment, bro."

I know he actually had good intentions when he said that to me because I was around him enough to understand he wasn't malicious, but it was still pessimistic advice. He was just projecting his insecurities on me. In his head, he thought he had no chance of getting with somebody like her, so he would have never even tried just to avoid being let down.

I made that girl my girlfriend about three weeks later.

Thinking somebody is out of your league is such a loser's mentality. It's like thinking, "why should I play if I'm going to lose?" If you think you're going to lose before you even play, then you're right; you're already a loser who doesn't value their worth.

In life, you don't lose from trying or failed attempts; you only lose from not trying or not learning from an experience.

Rejection could hurt, but going through life not doing what you want to do or not pursuing what you want to pursue because of the fear of rejection is for cowards. Fear should never be the obstacle that prevents you from going after what you want. With time, that will make you bitter and envious towards people that actually go after what they want because those people eventually obtain most of what they're after.

Also, the hurt of rejection is not that big of a deal—it's always a bigger deal in your imagination than actual reality, and all successful people understand that rejection is a part of the journey to success.

You will never have what you wish to obtain from life by giving just one bat at it, let alone none; THAT IS A RIDICULOUS WAY OF THINKING!

Don't let emotions control your intellect

I graduated from Bogan High School, located on the south side of Chicago at 79th and Pulaski. Bogan was a school mixed with mostly blacks and Latinos, and it wasn't very prestigious. We actually had to go through metal detectors every morning to ensure our safety, and we had enough security to start a football team (slight exaggeration but barely) because fights could break out at any given moment the second you stepped in those doors.

I know this school sounds horrible, and I'd be lying if I said it taught me much academically, but it did offer me many experiences I've come to appreciate.

During my junior year, I often ditched my math class to sneak into the cafeteria.

My math class was wild! Kids throwing books at each other for fun, blasting music, messing with the teacher, and smoking weed out of a window. Yes, smoking weed out of a window.

That environment didn't necessarily bother me, but sometimes it could get annoying, so I preferred to go to the cafeteria to hang out with one of my friends.

The first time I snuck into the cafeteria during that period, I was introduced to the people my friend would sit with, and that's where I met the first love of my life, Paloma.

Paloma was a light-skinned brunette, about five feet, six inches tall, with a slim stomach and a fat ass. She had a friendly smile, and her dark brown eyes had a spark of innocence to them. Her nose was medium-sized with not a lot of volume to her bridge.

I knew Paloma already, but the first time I talked to her was that day, and we clicked right off the bat.

Being around Paloma felt so right from the start, and although she was attractive to me, there wasn't an instant desire to make her my girlfriend. It was just cool going to her lunch period to hang out with her and my boy to avoid going to my math class.

Eventually, though, the male instinct in me kicked in, so I started thinking, "Damn! Paloma got a fat ass — maybe I should try to get at her."

I began flirting with Paloma by complimenting her a lot and getting touchy — playing games like thumb wrestle and slaps. (Yes, that worked for me then)

As the year moved forward, we started walking each other to our classes more often, and things just kept escalating after that.

She became my girlfriend close to the end of junior year, and we dated for about six months — until I decided to break up with her.

You see, those six months were nice, but I just simply didn't want to be in a relationship anymore.

When we broke up the first time, I went on vacation to Mexico right after.

Worst fucking vacation I've ever had! I just wanted to be around her. Not being around Paloma's energy made me feel miserable the whole time I was there.

As soon as I got back to Chicago, I talked to Paloma to find out if she was still interested in me, but she didn't give me a clear response.

Around this time, the school decided to form a Latino dance group. Paloma joined, and so did I. Of course, I asked her to be my partner, and although she showed a little reluctance, she agreed.

To me, this was an opportunity to get her to "like me" again, and so I started trying to win her back by doing things outside of the time we spent together dancing.

She liked this Frappuccino from Starbucks called "Java Chip," so I got her one every other practice. Sometimes, I would also write Facebook statuses with song lyrics or indirect expressions I knew would catch her attention.

Slowly but surely, she began to show interest in me once again.

When Valentine's Day came around the corner, I bought her a teddy bear. One of her friends gave me her lock combination, and so I got to school that day really early to shove the teddy bear in there with a note that said, "Let's talk after school."

When we met up after classes, we small-talked as we walked outside of the school. When we stopped walking, I looked her dead in the eyes, and I said, "Look, I know we broke up, so things aren't probably going to be the same if we get back together, but I promise you I will try my best for them to be better."

And things did get a whole lot better.

Paloma stimulated my sexual desire to a very intense level after we got back together. At that time, I drove a Tahoe and so when we spent time outside of school, we parked every opportunity we could, kissing and touching each other erratically.

We became so passionate about showing each other affection that she would even sometimes touch me inappropriately when I would be over her parents' house while they were there.

She would look at me with this sexy look, biting her index finger, challenging me to touch her back. When I said "Stop," she would tease me and poke fun of my masculinity by replying things like, "Make me" with a flirty smile. (Technically, today in 2021, that would be harassment because verbally I said "stop," and she said "no" and actually shamed me for saying no, but it really wasn't the case. My head was over the clouds for this girl.)

As time went on, I started to develop deeper and deeper emotions for Paloma, and it began to scare me.

It scared me because being in a serious relationship is still not what I wanted at eighteen—not even after falling in love for the first time.

About eleven months into the relationship, I decided to break up with Paloma a second time, then, about a month later, I tried getting her back a third time.

She didn't even want to hear what I had to say. She didn't want to talk on the phone or reply to any of my messages, and I had no idea how to meet up with her because school was over, and her friends didn't want to help me connect with her anymore.

"Luckily" for me, though, she was friends with this one guy named Javier, who was my friend as well, but more so hers. Thanks to the "guy code" and my persuasion skills, Javier set her up so I could meet up with her.

He asked her if she was home because he wanted to drop something off for her. When she said she was, I pulled up to the front of her house and decided to knock on her door.

My heart was beating really fast before knocking, and when I did, her mother was the one to answer the door. Paloma was right behind her mom, and both of their faces looked surprised and confused to see me.

There was a slight moment of awkward silence until I said to her mom, "Hi, can you give Paloma permission to talk to me for a bit?"

Her mom apologized to me and said she was busy at the moment. Then she closed the door slowly on me as she still looked surprised and confused.

The emotional pain I experienced after that was something my body wasn't familiar with, so later at night, that same day, I went for a ride and parked my car somewhere low-profile to allow myself to cry.

In my head, around that time, I would have said anything, done anything if Paloma was willing to give me just one more chance. I would have married her if that's what it took for us to get back together, and so today I'm glad she decided not to talk to me that day.

Then, I didn't understand the procedure of overcoming a breakup or how to handle the pain, so going back to her is what made the most sense.

I was willing to make irrational decisions like marrying at seventeen, not because I had changed my mind about wanting to commit to her at the time. I was willing to make such decisions because I wanted my pain to go away.

You can't trust your emotions when your heart is broken. "Brain studies have shown that withdrawals from romantic love activate the same mechanism in our brain that gets activated when addicts are withdrawing from substances like cocaine or opioids."

Trusting your emotions while being heartbroken is like trusting a drug addict with your money.

The longer you've been with somebody, the smaller the odds become of either one having the courage to make the decision to completely split up.

I'm not encouraging anybody to split up as soon as an inconvenience happens in their relationship. Disagreements are bound to happen, even in healthy relationships. However, I am encouraging people to split up when they know they should no longer be in that relationship and the reason they decide to stay with somebody is due to an emotional decision and not a rational one.

Majority of people who get married get divorced or live unhappily with their significant other. That is not because love isn't powerful, but because too many people make emotional decisions instead of rational ones when it comes to choosing or deciding to stay with a partner.

Always try to remember not to make emotional decisions that aren't paired with rationality — you will be more than likely to regret them in the long run, even if those emotional decisions pertain to love.

Love is not the only factor that will determine your happiness in this life, so be very careful about making decisions based solely on your emotions.

Enjoy being single and accept when you're not

I give huge props to people who have married their high school sweethearts and live happily in a healthy relationship.

To me, being in a relationship with somebody you love is better than being single. However, being single can be amazing as well, and I'm glad I have been able to experience a whole lot of it.

I doubt I would have appreciated Paloma the way she needed to be appreciated as my partner if I had stayed with her that early in my life.

In retrospect, it would have been hard for me to accept I had lost a lot of my freedom at seventeen. I needed to experience life on my own for a while, not only to be sure what it was I really wanted out of life but also to enjoy myself without any restrictions, including having sex with multiple women.

Being single has given me full freedom to go and do whatever I want without feeling like I owe anybody an explanation about anything. It feels really good to have had the opportunity to experience that because when you decide to settle down with somebody, doing whatever you feel like doing will cost you, and rightfully so.

When you decide to be with a person exclusively, you have to understand that some of your actions will affect your partner. You are no longer accountable for just your emotions. You are no longer entitled to all of your freedom.

Some might argue you shouldn't lose any of your freedom when you're in a relationship, but the reality is you will. You cannot expect to live life as if you're not committed to somebody while being committed to someone. That is the perfect way to set a romantic relationship up for failure.

So, if you decide to settle down with somebody early in your life, that's fine, but you have to understand and accept you're giving up some of your freedom.

SIDE NOTE: Just because you don't have all of your freedom when in a monogamist relationship does not mean you should lose all of your freedom either. Losing some of your freedom to cope with each other's emotions is not the same as being in a controlling relationship. Those are two different things.

This section is not intended to point out the boundaries you should have with your significant other, you guys have to decide those for yourselves. Communicating and acknowledging each other's emotions with LOGIC and CLARITY will lead to a healthier relationship.

This section is intended to make you step back and analyze if you're really ready to be in a relationship or in a serious commitment with anybody.

Romance isn't enough to maintain a healthy relationship

At the age of twenty, I began working as a food runner at Willow Room restaurant in an area up north called Lincoln in Chicago.

I had worked on the North side of Chicago before, washing dishes, but would only talk to the Mexican cooks. I would do my job, get my money, and rush back to the south side.

The south side is where I lived and the people you met from other races other than black and Latino were handpicked.

Working as a food runner made me interact a lot more with the staff of other ethnicities, cultures, etc., which introduced me to a new environment I liked very much.

It only got better when I met the most beautiful white girl my eyes had ever seen, Nina.

Nina was the hostess there. She was a five feet seven inches blonde with an amazing body. She had colored eyes and a very pretty smile. (It is rare for me to crush on anybody, and I definitely had a thing for this girl.)

Initially, I wasn't completely sure if I should make a move on somebody I was going to have to keep working with, but in retrospect (as corny as it might sound), I think we were just bound to happen.

It didn't take long for us to begin flirting with one another. We would play around all the time and make bets during work on how long it would take for tables to leave or how many reservations we would get overall at the end of the day.

In about a month, she owed me $100. I really was just betting with her as an excuse to always keep engaged with her presence, so I told her she didn't have to pay me. Still, she insisted on honoring her bet. I suggested she take me out for drinks instead, and she agreed. (I know I don't sound like a gentleman, but trust me, she came up more than $100 on me looking back on our relationship.)

The night we went out for drinks, I wasn't sure what to expect, but it was very nice. We had a really good time at the bar we went to, and after, we walked around outside for a few minutes before ordering my Uber.

Later, when my Uber arrived, she leaned over and gave me a goodbye kiss. After that night and a couple more lovely dates, we soon became boyfriend and girlfriend.

My relationship with Nina started off great, as majority of relationships do. And as I'm writing this, aside from my mother and sister, she has been the woman I've come to love the most on this earth, but our relationship became complicated.

Our relationship was complicated because the relationship I had with myself at the time was not pretty. There was so much going on in my life, and it often reflected on our relationship because I was not dealing with a lot of it properly.

Your relationships will always be complicated if you don't have a good relationship with yourself. It does not matter how great things kick off or how much love you develop for one another. Romance won't be enough to maintain a healthy relationship.

There is nothing wrong with failed relationships — failed relationships can teach you plenty. Nonetheless, when you're actually serious about building a solid relationship with somebody, you have to start by building a solid relationship with yourself.

The best way to develop a solid relationship with yourself is to first acknowledge what it is that's wrong with you.

Not acknowledging your issues is the easiest way to create more.

Find out what your addictions and/or bad habits are

We all have addictions and/or bad habits. Some people's issues are more severe than others. Some people will never accept that they have any issues to prevent themselves from starting any change, and especially if the word *addiction* is attached to those issues.

The word addiction is scary and most people would prefer not to attach it to their character. I don't have a problem attaching it to mine if it can help others accept their truth.

To be addicted means to have a physical and mental dependence on something, according to oxford languages. The keyword to identify addiction is dependency.

I'm addicted to two things, and possibly a third, but the third can be debatable to determine if it's an addiction or just a bad habit.

Getting coffee at least once a day is a must for me. I can't remember a time I went more than twenty-four hours without caffeine. I have tried to substitute this intake with tea, but the most I have ever gone without coffee is three weeks.

My second addiction is two things together: masturbation and pornography. I can't remember a time I went four weeks straight without masturbation since I found out about it, and the longest I've gone without watching porn is about a month.

The third thing and the most destructive for me out of the three is alcoholism.

The reason I say it's debatable whether it is an addiction or just a bad habit is because my dependency on it could be uncertain. Nevertheless, it's been the biggest factor in the problems in my life and the people around me.

I know most of Tip's (Best friend from high school) family because I would go over to his house often (mostly for family reunions).

In these reunions is where I met Jordan, Tip's cousin. He was a five feet eight inches light-skinned Mexican. He weighed about one hundred and eighty pounds and had an athletic body.

Jordan, Tip, a guy named Nando, and I became really close friends when I was turning nineteen.

Nando went to high school with Tip and I. Nando was about Jordan's stature and was also a light-skinned

Mexican, except he weighed about twenty pounds more than Jordan.

Our relationship developed when we all decided to join the gym. There we would sit and talk bullshit in the locker room more than we would actually work out. Aside from our stupid sense of humor, the next best thing that got us to be really close was the drinking habit we picked up. I say we picked up because I noticed how our drinking escalated throughout time. I'm not relating my personal vices/experiences with alcohol with their own, but it is a fact that all of our consumption of alcohol increased through time.

Our routine slowly, but surely consisted of drinking on the weekends and talking about what we would drink during the weekend throughout our week while we "worked out." There were plenty days when we would be in the locker room and decide to exit the gym to go drinking instead. (We thought it was hilarious.)

Jordan was the guy I did most of my early partying with because he was always down to go anywhere with me. He was a good-looking man, and I'm convinced we would have gotten with a lot more attractive girls if he had a little more game. You see, Jordan had some game, but he was always trying to be too funny, and his English wasn't very good. In other words, he was the master of talking himself out the pussy that was constantly thrown at him. We had serious conversations at times, but our time together consisted of who could say the next dumbest thing to make each other laugh the hardest.

Nando was my right-hand guy. He had a girlfriend in Mexico the whole time after high school, so he didn't really go to house parties with Jordan and me. But he was always down for Tip's family reunions or close friend gatherings, where I did majority of my drinking.

Getting really comfortable with these peers made it too easy for me to pick up a drinking habit. It also made it hard for me to realize I was picking up a bad habit because they were good people, and we were just drinking to have a good time.

Bad habits and addictions are easy to develop, but they're hard to get rid of, especially when you won't acknowledge they are addictions or bad habits.

Acknowledging and accepting what your addictions and bad habits are will lead you to a better life.

Of course, some addictions are not as bad as others if you look at them objectively. But as human beings, we are incredibly good at looking for confirmation and validation when it comes to the things we want to believe.

You won't ever work on something you don't perceive as a problem. Still, if you're reading this, it is time to stop tricking yourself about the benefits certain habits and addictions provide for you if they constantly leave you in compromised predicaments.

Your lifestyle depends on your choices, even if your circumstances make it seem like it doesn't

My brother is four years younger than me. He is a tan skinny Mexican boy, weighs about one hundred thirty-five pounds, and measures five feet nine inches. He has light brown eyes, black wavy hair, thick eyebrows, a slim smooth face, and medium-sized lips.

We grew up in the same household. He has always had a very chill, reserved personality (when he is not intoxicated). And we have a good relationship for the most part, but it got shaky for a while at the beginning of 2016 when I was twenty years old.

This happened when my mother found out he started smoking marijuana at the age of sixteen. He probably started earlier, but that's when my mother found out. (In a Mexican household, finding out your sixteen-year-old smokes marijuana can become a big deal.) I'm not implying marijuana is the reason issues begin to occur, but from that moment on is when I remember the lives of my immediate family beginning to complicate more and more.

There was a local "gang" in the neighborhood we lived in at the time, and my brother began hanging out with that crowd. I use quotations for the word gang because it's a small number of members compared to the average number of members belonging to other gangs in Chicago.

My brother never joined that gang, but he was around them often. When my parents found out about the people he was hanging out with, it affected them, but mostly my mother. She lost a lot of weight, and all she seemed to be focused on was attempting to ensure that my brother distanced himself from such companions and bad habits.

While I was sleeping, my little brother would often come home intoxicated, either from alcohol, weed, both, or maybe even other things. This was a tough time for me because when I heard my parents lecturing him, all I thought to do was beat some sense into him to make better decisions, but my mother always demanded I do not interfere.

One day while I was working, a guy I knew sent me a video through Facebook messenger. This video was of two teens who were walking together. In this clip, you can see teen number one get punched in his head from behind by some random male, while teen number two took off running the moment this happened. After teen number one gets hit from behind, he falls on the floor, and then you can see various males rushing to stomp him out repeatedly.

My brother was teen number two, who was captured making a run.

I still remember how my blood boiled when I saw that video. Seconds after it finished, I asked one of my boys to let me borrow his strap (gun). I was ready to put a bullet in somebody; I just had to be sure who these people were.

When the information got back to me, a lot of shit just didn't add up. Some people claimed it was some boys from a different gang, another one of my boys said it was a crew from back in the days. So, somehow, it was all these different people that had done it. And although I'm good at playing stupid, the reality is I'm far from it.

Moments like this made me realize little by little that the street's code of ethics was built to hold us minorities back in life. But it is still up to us to decide if we are going to fall for the bullshit or not.

To me, it's understandable why some people get caught up in that lifestyle. However, the code of "ethics" behind it makes no logical sense.

The streets will label you pussy for running away from a bunch or random people that pulled up on you unexpectedly, then those same people will never address a bunch of people by themselves or without a gun. The streets will trick you into thinking it's pussy not to have the heart to kill another person and make an innocent mother suffer. The streets will trick you into thinking there is honor in waiting for you to die to "honor" your name by killing somebody in your name. The streets will really trick you into thinking there is pride in allowing others to whoop your ass to belong into something—something where you constantly need to prove yourself to other males by taking loss after loss.

Be very careful making decisions that will lead you to a lifestyle where every decision leaves you in a losing situation.

You should understand that you choose your way of living and every decision you make is on you. Your circumstances will always test you, but it's up to you to choose how you want to live YOUR life.

If I had decided to attempt to murder somebody based on my current situation, my life would be worse, and it would have been because of a decision I decided to make, not the circumstance at hand.

Strong-minded individuals don't allow their circumstances to dictate their fate, no matter the odds stacked against them. Fuck any lifestyle of hate, fear, and insecurities driven by fragile, bruised egos.

"You can be smart and make stupid decisions, but you must not be smart if you keep making decisions you know are stupid." - Francisco Gallardo

---

SIDE NOTE: For too long, it felt like it was my responsibility to guide my brother through the right path or to "protect" him, and it was draining me.

We have to understand that other people's decisions are not our responsibility. It's good to attempt to influence people to do better, but we shouldn't persist on anybody to do anything. It's hard to understand that when you feel you know what's best for somebody you love, but that's not often the best for yourself or that relationship. You have to allow people the freedom to figure it out on their own.

Don't mix alcohol with your emotional instability

A little before turning twenty-one, I decided to move away from home and rent an apartment with my sister, who is two years older than me.

As I look back at my life, I was not emotionally stable from nineteen to twenty-one, but there was a lot to learn from those years.

Thanks to the acknowledgment of my bad habits; I have also realized the danger of mixing liquor with emotional instability.

Drinking while not being in a good state of mind will often bring up all the emotions you're bottling inside and not dealing with properly. And let me tell you, that shit will not be pretty.

One night, I decided to bring my brother around my group of friends when we went drinking at Tip's brother's house. (In my head, bringing him around my friends would discourage him from hanging out with his group of friends.)

I began drinking a lot that night, and so did my brother. We had a good time until we left the reunion. When we stepped outside, before getting in the car, we started arguing about something. Nina (my girlfriend at the time) was with me that day, and since she was sober, she drove us home. The argument continued throughout the ride home until we parked outside the apartment. When we got out of the car, he refused to go inside the apartment building and began walking in the opposite direction. While screaming at him to come back, I started walking towards him. Then he swung at me, hitting me straight in the face. I reacted by hitting him in return, punching his jaw and knocking him out cold. When he was on the floor, I carried him with his belly on my shoulder while holding his thighs with both of my arms locked together. As I struggled to walk to the apartment with him, the police showed up. They handcuffed me with my face against the hood of the cop car, and they put my brother inside the car.

A couple tears shed down my cheeks while being handcuffed, but not because I was handcuffed or because I had my face to the hood of the car—I was mentally drained and I hated what my life was becoming. There were too many emotions bottled inside I was not dealing with properly. The only way I was allowing myself to express those emotions was after reaching a level of intoxication where I became oblivious to my consciousness.

Alcohol is a tricky substance. It is a central nervous system depressant, meaning that it slows down brain functioning and neural activity. Regardless, it is socially acceptable to abuse this substance as long as we have a designated driver. It is heavily influenced to drink this substance, not just by companies selling it but friends and often, even by family. Sometimes, even by people like myself that have experienced more than one similar story like the one I just shared.

Most people will refuse to look at the pros and cons of alcohol objectively because when you're hooked on a substance, it's incredibly hard to be unbiased.

This section is not intended to convince anybody who doesn't believe they have a problem with drinking to stop drinking. You have to decide what's bad for you by yourself. However, I'm hoping if you're reading this and can relate at least a little bit, maybe you'll self-reflect and think twice before drinking alcohol while not being in a good place with yourself.

Separate from friends that don't make your life better

Super bowl 2018, I got drunk at Tip's brother's house and made a scene.

His house was a single home divided into three sections: the basement, main floor, and the attic.

There were about ten other people there that night, including my girlfriend at the time, Nina. After the football game, half of the people were hanging out in the main section of the house. Nando, Jordan, Tip, Tip's nephew, and I decided to go to the attic for a bit.

There, we began playing wrestling like little ass kids. The rules were that you had to make your opponent tap out to take the win. I went up against Tip's nephew. He was probably fifteen or sixteen year's old, but about fifteen pounds heavier than me.

When we went at it, Jordan proclaimed I tapped out.

I said, "What the fuck are you talking about, Jordan? Jordan a blind motherfucker, let's go again."

The boy said, "Okay, hold up, let me catch my breath, though."

I replied, saying, "Na, let's get it right now, boy."

After saying that, everybody said, "Let's just go downstairs and get a beer," because they could tell I was getting heated.

I replied, "I'll go downstairs in a minute, Ima chill up here for a bit."

Tip decided to stay up with me.

As I was catching my breath, Tip grabbed my shirt and said, "Paco, I love you, but you need to chill bro, this is my brother's house."

I replied, "Ima count to three, and you better let go of my shirt, or Ima smack yo ass."

Tip replied, "I would never hit you back bro, I love you too much…."

As he was still holding on to my shirt, talking to me, I punched him in his mouth and said, "Motherfucker, I told you to let go of my shirt."

After hitting him, I went downstairs and yelled, "Nina, let's go!"

Everybody looked confused about my behavior. Then some people started asking what was going on.

Frustrated, I tried to explain what was going on.

Tip's brother then cut me off and said, "Alright! You need to calm down."

When I heard that, I yelled at Nina again while looking at him, "Nina, let's go before I make a scene up in here" (as I was already making a scene).

Telling a male that's drunk, upset, and full of testosterone to calm down is like smacking a pit bull you don't own and expecting him to sit down.

When we walked out of the house, Nando came out to try and understand what was going on. It was February in Chicago, so it was a little cold. When he asked what was going on, I started to curse him out for no reason.

I got in his face and said something along the lines of, "The fuck you coming out here for? You should have had my back in there, now everybody looking at me crazy, man fuck you, go inside pussy!"

Nina went to grab my wrist tight, rushing us both to leave, so I started walking away from Nando while still indirectly talking shit.

Then, after walking a few steps, I decided to snatch my hand away from Nina aggressively to walk back towards Nando. When I got close enough, I mushed him in the face and tried to get him to fight me, but he didn't engage. He just stared at me in a confused and disappointed manner, then I finally walked away, feeling no type of remorse.

Two reasons to share that story:

I. Emphasize that mixing alcohol with your emotional instability is not a good idea.

II. Help you understand that sometimes you need to separate from certain friends to make it easier on YOURSELF to seek a better lifestyle.

It is true, that group of friends and I parted ways because I was out of hand that night, and not because of a conscious decision beforehand, but it doesn't have to be that way for you. You don't have to wait for shit to hit the fan to separate from a lifestyle you're not benefiting from.

I have amazing memories with those people I will always cherish, and yes, I was a bad friend that night for wilding out, but our separation served me really well.

These individuals were good people and fun to be around, but in retrospect, I did not like our way of living as much, and I needed to get away from it if I ever wanted to obtain one that I really did.

Our routines consisted of working out mediocrely, playing soccer mediocrely, but drinking at a professional level.

We would get together during the weekend at one of Tip's family member's house or go to a local brewery and just get drunk.

For starters, I don't even like craft beer, and although Tip's family was great, there are so much more things I want to do in my twenties than sit around at somebody's house every weekend to drink beer.

To be clear, I am not, and I will never blame them for MY bad decisions or the drinking habit I picked up. Every wrong decision I have made is on me. No one forced me to make wrong decisions, and this book is meant to influence better decisions than the ones I've made. But they were the reason picking up that bad habit became easier for me, and it would have been harder for me to stay away from liquor while still being really close to them or while continuing to be close to such routine.

Remember that your lifestyle depends on your choices, even if your circumstances make it seem like it doesn't.

In the past two years, I have met new individuals who are cool, and if I had not separated from that group of friends, it would have been very difficult to allow myself time for anybody outside of the persons who were already in my life. That is not the case anymore, and trust me, sometimes it is good to mingle outside your comfort zone. New friends can teach you new things, and sometimes, they might even have better intentions than somebody you've known your whole life.

People you have become comfortable with might not always be the best fit for the lifestyle you're seeking or the evolution you're trying to obtain. It is up to YOU to change YOUR lifestyle and make better decisions, even if one of those decisions means separating from certain friends you've grown accustomed to.

SIDE NOTE: Keep in mind that more than one thing can always be true. You can still get better and work on yourself while remaining friends with somebody. Some people are really worth keeping in your life, and they might be trying to help you while you might be the one not helping yourself.

Also, even though it might be good to separate from certain friends, it does not mean you have to cut them off completely or end on bad terms. This particular situation with that group of friends ended badly for me, but it doesn't always have to, and I'm glad most of them never have.

Aside from making new friends in the last two years, I also reunited with many old ones, which felt really good. Even though we separated from each other at some point in our lives, there is still love, and it's nice to catch up here and there.

You don't have to be as involved as you once were in each other's life to still care and show love. It is also okay not to care anymore and just move on, but separating doesn't always have to mean never speaking again or holding grudges.

Holding grudges is not part of growing up.

Your perspective is your strongest weapon

According to what I hear and some things I have seen, both of my grandfathers were alcoholics.

My mom's father had a stroke that paralyzed half of his body, so, as of now, he can't overdrink even if he wanted to.

My dad's father loves shooting pool, and drinking just goes with it.

My father has been sober for many years now, but he used to be a heavy drinker as well.

I am extremely proud of my dad for becoming sober, and I often thank God for it.

I do not know how to drink alcohol moderately. If I have a drink, my chances of ending up drunk are very high. Certain friends tell me they enjoy my drunk personality, but I am not sure my family or ex-girlfriend would agree with such a statement.

It could be debatable whether I'm an alcoholic or not, but the label of what to call me is the thing that matters the least because I have struggled with the intake of alcohol.

In 2018, I made an effort to stop drinking because I realized I did not like the person I would often turn into with liquor in my system.

My attempt only lasted about four months.

The idea of never being able to drink again just seemed impossible to me. I love going out, and majority of the activities I enjoy doing also involve drinking. To me, never drinking again was equivalent to limiting my fun forever. It also meant never tasting great flavors again, such as a cold beer or a glass of wine.

People are often quick to equate not controlling your alcohol intake with a lack of self-control. And while they are not necessarily wrong, that's just such a simplistic way of looking at things.

Not drinking requires self-control, but using self-control to moderate your drinking or not drinking at all might be very difficult, even for somebody who doesn't lack self-control.

In December 2020, I published the first edition of this book. As I am re-writing this section, I have not drunk liquor for eight months now. The big difference between my last attempt and now is that I am not craving the taste of alcohol or the sensation of feeling drunk.

Not feeling like I have to continually use self-control to stop myself from consuming something I crave has helped me immensely.

If you're somebody who has struggled with alcohol intake, you might be wondering, "How?" And it's simple. I have changed my perspective on the "benefits" liquor was offering me by analyzing them.

About a year ago, if somebody asked me, "Do you like beer?" my response would be, "Absofuckinglutely!" Today that would no longer be my response.

The taste of beer is still cool to me, but that's because I practically forced myself into liking the flavor.

The first time I drank a full beer was in eighth grade. I mostly drank it because I didn't want to seem like a little bitch for not finishing it in front of my friends, but the taste was disgusting. The more I drank, the more I got used to the flavor, and I eventually started to enjoy it. (If you have to force a substance down your throat the first five times, chances are that the flavor is just not as good as you want to make it out to be.)

What I was never able to develop a taste for was straight liquor. Tequila, whiskey, cognac, etc., have always tasted extremely disgusting to me. There was a time when I would be like, "Yeah, I like Jameson shots," but I was lying, not just to other people but to myself. What I really should have said was, "Jameson is the least disgusting, so I'll drink that." But, to me, admitting to myself, or anybody else, that liquor was disgusting wasn't even an option.

It wasn't an option because, although I hated the taste of liquor, I loved the idea of having a conversation about liquor preference, taking shots, and getting drunk.

The idea of taking shots has always been really cool to me because it's a way to bond with others and celebrate. But never in my life have I taken a shot and said, "God, that was some good flavor." On the contratry, I have vomited after taking so many shots and made many sour faces as if I had taken a big bite out of a lime. And this isn't just a 'me thing; I have observed many people that swear to love liquor do sour faces all the time and throw up, even when most shots served at bars are no more than two ounces.

Is it natural to make a sour face after consuming two ounces of any type of liquid if you really enjoy it? Of course not, unless you're lying to yourself about liking the flavor, or if you're in the process of forcing yourself into liking the flavor.

"Well, Paco, liquor is sour just like lime. Does that mean you don't enjoy lime?"

I enjoy lime, but I will never drink two ounces of lime juice and describe it as "tasteful." That would be idiotic.

So, as of right now, I've been doing fine without the taste of liquor overall. And even though I have developed a taste for beer (by practically forcing myself to), if I really crave the flavor alone, I can just buy some Heineken zero (non-alcoholic beverage), which tastes just like regular Heineken. But if I'm being completely honest, I don't really crave the flavor itself that often or intensely. Majority of the time I actually decide to grab a six pack of non-alcoholic beverages, is when I go to functions. And half of the time, it has more to do with blending in with the environment than actually wanting to satisfy my craving for the taste.

Now, of course, flavor isn't the only factor as to why I drank excessively, but the feeling.

"When you drink alcohol, you increase the release of dopamine in the brain's reward center. By increasing dopamine levels in your brain, alcohol tricks the brain into thinking you feel great." And who the fuck doesn't like to feel great? I definitely do, except the lowest moments in my life have happened while being drunk.

The more liquor I consume, the more I lose self-awareness and self-control. This means I am more likely to do something embarrassing, impulsive, or out of my character (like acting foul towards the people I love).

You often hear people say things like, "Drunk people and children are the most honest people on Earth." And while that saying sounds good, it's really stupid. "Alcohol suppresses our inhibition and triggers emotional reactions. It affects the parts of the brain controlling movement, speech, judgment, and memory (self-awareness and self-control)." Suppose your way of describing an honest person is somebody with slowed reflexes, slurred speech, poor judgment, and a blurred memory; in that case, that's fine, but to me, it doesn't seem logical to believe or trust anything from a person in such a condition.

The more I have played devil's advocate to think about a good reason why the sensation of alcohol is worth it for me, the more I've convinced myself that it just isn't.

Aside from liquor stripping me away from self-awareness and self-control (two of the things I'm most proud to have a lot of) in exchange for a few hours of "fun," it also makes me feel like shit the following day.

After turning twenty-three, my hangovers began to last for too long. Not only did I start having strong headaches, but my anxiety would be through the roof, and I would feel depressed for a whole day. A WHOLE FUCKING DAY.

For a long time, it felt like the overconsumption of alcohol was worth it. After analyzing the benefits that substance was providing me with, I've realized I could do just fine without those benefits.

I will continue to go out and have fun because I love that, but going out to have fun looks different for me now.

Being eight months without drinking liquor has prevented me from hanging out with certain people as much as I used to. This is not because being sober limits how much fun I have while being out, but because I've realized that those people are not that exciting to be around, and being sober limits how much fun I have around them.

If I feel bored around a person now, my logic isn't that it's because I'm not drinking. No, my logic is that it's because they're not fun to be around unless I'm drunk out of my mind. And frankly, my personality in general is too dope to be wasted around boring people.

Even with my closest friends, I don't stay out late as often. This is not because they're not exciting to be around, but because sometimes they become boring and even embarresing after consuming too much liquor. If you think I'm exaggerating simply to make a point, try having a conversation with any drunk person while being sober. You won't only notice they'll spit saliva at you while they're talking, but their conversation will be difficult to follow because of how unarticulate their sentences have become.

If you're reading this and might not relate to this section because you have your drinking under control, here's something to consider: In my years of mingling around drunks, I've yet to meet one with a "drinking problem", they all got it "under control." And no, I'm not implying everyone who drinks has a drinking problem, there is some people who understand how to use the substance as oppose to the substance using them. Still, alcohol is a progressive drug and I am saying most of you are full of shit when it comes to being honest to yourselves about how much control it has over you, and the fact that it is socially acceptable to abuse this substance allows many of you to hide behind that.

SIDE NOTE: This section was inspired by a book I read called "The Easy Way to Control Drinking" by Allen Carr. I hope this section is of some help to anybody, but I must be clear that my book is not a guide on how to control your drinking if you struggle with alcoholism, it's just my perspective and what seems to work for ME.

Holding somebody unstable down will hold both of you back

Nina was there for me while I struggled with my personal issues. She helped me so much through this time, and I'm thankful for it, but at some point, it began to hold both of us back too.

When I dated Nina, she disclosed to me she dealt with anxiety, and around that time, I just couldn't wrap my head around the concept of that. I thought she was just exaggerating and being overly emotional most of the time because I was not in the state of mind to sympathize, let alone empathize with such emotions. The only advice I could give out was the best advice given to me growing up, to "man up."

Our last fight was ugly. It started with a disagreement, and it kept escalating. I remember telling her I was tired of her using her "anxiety" as an attempt to make me feel bad during arguments. With tears in her eyes, she began to scream at me—probably due to impotence—and so I screamed at her in return. I still remember how I felt no remorse screaming at her and seeing her cry.

It makes me very sentimental to write this because I should have given her a tight hug and try to understand what she was dealing with for once. But how could I when I couldn't even understand my fucking myself.

Even though my life would have been ten times harder without Nina around that time, at some point, we were no longer holding each other down—we were holding each other back.

Your relationships will always be healthier if you are. I keep saying this because it's worth memorizing. It is easier to work on your relationship when you at least understand your own issues.

Couples should be there for each other during hard times, but neither one is entitled to take advantage of another. When your significant other is facing something difficult, it is your duty to be there for them. You can HELP them overcome the situation or make it easier on them, but at no point should you let them take ADVANTAGE of you because of their struggles and circumstances.

SIDE NOTE: This is my experience, and I'm not saying you can't grow as a person while in a relationship. I encourage growth, always. What I am saying is to identify the difference in helping somebody trying to better themselves versus comforting somebody who continues to stay the same or get worse because they have no intention to better themselves.

It is time to move on if you constantly find yourself comforting somebody who has no intention of bettering themselves, because then, you will both be holding each other back.

Your breakups should make you better

You shouldn't let the pain of a breakup convince you to devalue yourself constantly. Ask yourself what you might have done wrong so you can grow as a person and attract a partner that suits you best, but don't dwell on what could have been or how life sucks after something didn't go the way you would have liked.

This book isn't for victims or people looking to justify their shitty lives based on their shortcomings—it's about learning from them.

Do not channel your energy into who you used to be, but rather who you can become.

You also shouldn't let the pain of a breakup have you hold resentment towards your ex-partner just because it didn't work out. At some point in life, you loved that individual.

The number of people I hear talking ill about people they claimed to once loved makes me sad because they let love turn into hate simply because the relationship didn't work out. And even if that person hurt you unrightfully, you shouldn't channel your energy into somebody who will no longer play a role in your life. Use all that pain to make yourself better, not bitter.

The pain of my breakups has been intense, but it has helped me become a much better person.

It is hard to be bitter towards others when you're at peace with yourself, especially towards anybody that has offered you amazing memories throughout life.

Acknowledge your mental health

Mental health has become a fascinating subject to me. Three years ago, though, I could not give a fuck about it.

Mental health was just not of my understanding. To me, there were strong-minded people, weak-minded people, and people who were fucked up.

Strong-minded people were the ones that knew how to "deal" (bottle up) with their issues. Weak-minded people did not know how to "deal" (bottle up) with their issues. And the people who were fucked up were the ones who were diagnosed with some sort of mental disorder by a professional.

If you are somebody with that similar mentality, it is time you allow yourself to grow through education.

Mental health can pertain to many things, being that it refers to a person's condition to their psychological and emotional well-being.

Anxiety is the mental health issue I will write on, being the one I am most knowledgeable about and the most relatable to my life. But, hopefully, reading about it will also help you realize the importance of understanding the idea of mental health in general.

As humans, it is normal to experience intense anxiety when we perceive a threat. Severe anxiety is meant to help our body react to that threat.

The explanation of this physiological reaction is referred to as the "fight or flight response."

The following is an oversimplified description of the anatomy process during this response: When you perceive danger or any stressful situation, that information gets sent to the amygdala, an area of the brain that contributes to emotional processing. If the amygdala perceives danger, it sends a distress signal to the hypothalamus (another part of the brain). The hypothalamus then sends signals to the rest of your body through the peripheral nervous system (sympathetic division), preparing it to either fight or flee. The way the sympathetic division prepares the body is by stimulating the adrenal glands. The adrenal glands then release hormones such as epinephrine (adrenaline) and Norepinephrine (noradrenaline) that will increase your strength and physical performance.

A hypothetical example/scenario that would trigger this process would be if you trespassed into somebody's property and heard/saw a grown pit bull barking at you. After identifying the pit bull as a threat, your anxiety would kick in. This will cause your adrenal glands to release hormones such as adrenaline and noradrenaline that will HELP you either fight or flee out of that dangerous situation.

It is normal for humans to feel some anxiety even when there is no actual physical threat around. Some might relate to feeling anxious if they have an assignment due the following day, interviewing for a new job position, thinking of or talking to somebody for the first time, etc.

Anxiety disorders are much more complex than that. People who deal with anxiety disorders constantly feel anxious.

The most common causes of extreme anxiety are inheritance, chemical imbalances in the brain, and experiences of traumatic events.

Despite not currently having resources to be diagnosed (like many minorities dealing with mental health issues), through reading and self-reflecting, I've realized that I deal with some sort of anxiety.

You would not know this unless I disclose it to you (as with the majority of people who deal with mental health issues) because I behave like a "normal" individual and not a "fucked-up one" throughout my day-to-day interactions.

My brain is very good at constantly creating hypothetical situations that can possibly leave me in bad predicaments. My anxiety heightens the possibility of the worst case scenarios in those situations actually happening if I don't react or plan for it in some sort of way. Sometimes, these thoughts can cause my heart rate to rise if I focus too much on them. Sometimes the negative outcomes I create in these hypothetical situations can be very unlikely to happen.

Feeling anxious has helped me out a lot to keep occupied doing productive things that might help me avoid ending in vulnerable situations. My fear of ending in bad predicaments or in a position where I have no control over an outcome has often pushed me to accomplish goal after goal, including writing this book.

This sounds really good, right? Except constantly having my brain working on solutions for problems can often cause me to feel extreme stress and frustration. Especially when I can't find a solution to a problem that might be a bigger deal in my head than actual reality.

When your brain functions in a constant state of worry, the release of stress hormones can be quite debilitating.

Acknowledging my mental health was crucial for me to understand myself to another level.

Before I clearly understood my anxiety, it was really easy for my frustration to turn into anger. Not actually knowing or inability to explain why I felt how I felt, often made me exaggerate any situation that might seem reasonable enough to be angry about because my body was in "fight" mode, full of hormones ready to be released (this is called Displacement in psychology, I would recommend you read about it).

Understanding my emotions better made me realize that most things I used to get frustrated about had less to do with anything other than my personal issues. And understanding this has made me deal with myself a lot better.

In the last two years, I've come to cope really well with my anxiety (you can read about this in the next section), but there are still certain situations that easily lead my thoughts to rise too high, making them really hard to control, causing me to have panic attacks.

Traveling by plane is an example of a situation that can easily make my thoughts rise uncontrollably.

Flying in a plane scares the living crap out of me. About two years ago, on my way back from Mexico, the pilot announced that two planes were next to ours, right before landing. Why did he announce this? I have no fucking idea. He was probably a pilot from Spirit. When he announced this, every muscle in my body tightened. To make things worse, the plane hit some turbulence, and the seat belt sign went off immediately after the announcement. In my head, I was convinced the other two planes had hit ours, and our plane was trying to land because we were at risk. Granted, we were just going in for a normal landing, but my thoughts and imagination were in overdrive. My heart was pumping incredibly fast. I was convinced if I didn't die due to a crash, I would die because of a heart attack, and there was nothing I could do to avoid either thing.

When we landed, my body was still shaking, and for the next two weeks, the muscles on my upper body's left side were very tight and uncomfortable.

Whenever I explain to people how much anxiety I get during flights, they say things like, "You just have to overcome it." "You just have to tell yourself that it is the safest form of transportation." Or "You need to focus on other things." Great advice, guys! Thank you! I don't know why I didn't think of that before!

I know I can't let fear stop me from living life, so I will always travel and work on overcoming my fears. Having said this, the process of doing so is not as easy as telling myself to overcome my fears. If this was the case, it wouldn't be an issue, to begin with. No matter what logical explanation I tell myself during a flight, my brain rejects it because being in a situation where I have no control to prevent possible negative outcomes raises my thoughts, causing me to have a panic attack.

The way I'd describe the feeling of a panic attack for me is a fear so intense that it feels as if I was facing an actual life or death experience, even if I really wasn't.

Anxiety is a prevalent mental health issue amongst society, but we don't often realize it because of our lack of education and the negative stigma behind such topic. This also means it is very likely that at least one of your family members struggles with some sort of anxiety or one of your friends, and it definitely does not mean they are "fucked up" or "weak-minded" individuals.

When I dated Nina, she disclosed she dealt with anxiety, so my first question was, "Did a doctor tell you this?" When she said, "No," my first thought was, "Ah shit, this girl might be a little weak-minded."

This way of thinking often caused me to be dismissive about her mental health, and ironically enough, about my own.

Unfortunately, most people are not prepared to handle a situation the way we would want them to, and a lot of the time, it's because those people are also dealing with something of their own they probably don't understand. It's hard to be empathetic when you can't even understand your own feelings.

Regardless, if you have something you are struggling with internally, it is always a good idea to seek help. Never assume your problems are not important to anybody. I probably won't know every single person that reads this. However, I still give a fuck, and that's part of why I'm writing, re-reading, and doing my best to articulate words that can help others.

For many people, mental health struggles are not easy to comprehend. Therefore, it is much easier to ignore them, dismiss them, or even criticize them. And while we don't need to understand every aspect of mental health to be better human beings, understanding its idea will make you a better person.

Educating yourself about mental health will lead you to have a better understanding of yourself and the people around you.

To anyone dealing with situations or emotions similar to mine, let me tell you it is okay you feel this way, and you can deal with these emotions, even if they're tough because you're tough as well. While it is not easy to work through these emotions or overcome these challenges, it is not impossible either.

Feeling fear can be embarrassing, and if you can't control it, it can make you feel like a weak individual. Hiding it does not make you stronger; it actually makes you more vulnerable. In all honesty, I don't like how it feels to share my struggles. Doing so makes me no longer appear to be Superman, and feeling vulnerable sucks! Having said this, we humans often need to feel vulnerable to change and evolve.

It's better to continue to get stronger while appearing weak than to get weaker while appearing to be strong.

Find out what works for you

Feeling fear is not a sign of weakness. It's incredibly normal and reasonable, but understanding this also shouldn't be an excuse for you not to work on these fears and figure out how to deal with them better.

The following is a list of free or economical options that help me cope with my mental health and can POSSIBLY help you too.

DRINKING: When I drink, I have zero anxiety because alcohol suppresses my fear, but if you read the past sections, you'll understand this is the worse way to cope with your mental health. Alcohol will not only reduce your anxiety for a very short period, but it's very likely to make your anxiety worse over time.

READING: Reading is the tool that educated me on mental health, helping me acknowledge my own.

Books are not that expensive. Look for what you like that might help you — there is a lot of options to choose from. If you don't know what you like, go and ask your friends, ask online, or go on YouTube. My favorite books were recommended through my favorite podcasters.

If you really don't have extra twenty to thirty dollars to spend, you can check something out for free at your local library. (Beggars can't be choosers either.)

SIDE NOTE: If you think this book can help somebody and you really don't have ten to fifteen dollars to spend, message me on my Instagram. (fgallardo_p)

LISTENING TO PODCAST: I was influenced to read about mental health by one of my favorite podcasters Charlamagne Tha God. Seeing that people with dope personalities also deal with mental health issues and support them, makes me feel better about myself.

Podcasts can be entertaining and educational. They are free on YouTube, and there is a variety of topics and people to choose from, so if you really take your time searching, there is a good chance you'll find something.

EXERCISING: Exercising does not only help me distract myself and feel better about my looks, but it also helps me release a lot of tension.

When I'm under a lot of stress now, I take it all out at the gym or playing a sport instead of dumping it on others. (This is called sublimation in psychology, I would recommend you read about it.)

Exercising can be expensive, but it is very economical, and it comes in different forms — soccer, basketball, boxing, lifting weights, etc. Find out what works for you.

TALKING: I understand our ego constantly fights us not to be vulnerable and disclose how we really feel, but Jay Z said it best, "You can't heal what you never revealed."

I enjoy talking in general because I'm a social person, but I'm referring to talking about emotions in this section. Talking to distract your mind and opening up about your feelings are not the same thing. They're both good, but it must be pointed out that majority of people are not equipped/prepared to listen to your shit, let alone give unbiased, logical feedback to your problems. Your partners, friends, relatives, etc., are not your therapist.

With that being said, I believe people should constantly find outlets where they can express their emotions without being judged.

I can't afford a psychologist yet, but I have been blessed to have somebody in my life to open up to that can understand me. When I open up about my emotion to this person, I feel enormous relief, and we all deserve to feel that.

LAUGHING: Laughing and not taking things too seriously is one of my favorite medicines. No matter how hard life gets, you will always see me trying to make others laugh or have a good time. If I took life as seriously as my problems, I would be depressed like a motherfucker.

If you are not one with a personality, then have others make you laugh. Stand-up comedy is free on YouTube, and if you have Netflix, there is a large variety of comedians to choose from.

ACCEPTING DEATH AND HAVING FAITH: In the past year, I've learned to accept I'm going to die. This doesn't mean I'm no longer afraid to die or by any means not trying to live, but I have trained my mind to feel ready for death.

Strengthening my spirituality has helped me a lot with this process. Having faith there is something good awaiting me after death brings me peace, and it often helps keep my thoughts from rising uncontrollably when I begin to feel too anxious.

Something that can make my anxiety worse is thinking I will die from a heart attack when my heart begins to feel an unusual heart rate. When I start to feel an unusual heart rate now, I just lean into the sensation and tell myself that if I die, everything will be okay because death is a part of life, and God really got me.

Entwined with faith is meditation for me. When I'm under a lot of stress, I like to go to a chapel in my old neighborhood and just sit still there for about ten minutes, trying to enjoy/focus on my breathing and the sound of whatever I'm able to hear in such a calm, peaceful place.

SINGING/DANCING: About twenty to twenty-five percent of my day is spent listening to music. Singing/rapping helps me feel alive. Singing or rapping lyrics I enjoy can change my mood in a matter of seconds.

I do less dancing than singing, but it is something that brings me joy as well.

Music is incredibly powerful!

Analyze your influences

Music is incredibly powerful — learn how to use that power.

My favorite genre in music is hip hop. I will use my favorite artists to deliver different messages within the message of this section.

FUCK A STREET MENTALITY

Street mentality: Way of thinking that glorifies the act of doing whatever means necessary to PROVE to yourself and others you are not soft or lame. (I will be using the following words under the context of this definition.)

Meek Mill is my fifth favorite artist.

When I would play Meek Mill's Intro, "Dreams and nightmares" at sixteen years old, I wanted to be a street dude so bad. Singing, "Real nigga what up, real nigga what up, if you ain't about that murder gang, then pussy nigga shut up" made me want somebody to try me, so I could kill them and feel like I'm not a pussy or somebody to fuck with. Only for a few minutes, though, because then I'd start thinking rationally and see how that might sound cool, but it's really stupid.

I know, to a chunk of people reading this, me saying, "Then I'd start thinking rationally and see how that might sound cool, but it's really stupid" sounds like common sense. Still, to some people who grow up in rough environments with no solid role models other than their favorite rappers, that mentality is cool and not stupid at all.

The street violence aspect of hip-hop culture has contributed to keeping many of us dumb down in society. Constantly hearing lyrics like the one I just quoted by Meek has helped reinforce the street mentality, but it must be said that this is not hip-hop's fault; it is our fault, the listeners'.

I would never vouch for an artist or a genre to switch THEIR content when it comes to music. Artists should not be restricted when it comes to their art. But as listeners, we must learn how to compartmentalize what is worth taking in from music.

In this world, there will always be bad you can get through the good, and good you can get through the bad. And fuck adopting or reinforcing a street mentality through hip-hop—there are so many more positive things you can get out of it.

"I gotta inspire them, motivate the people where I come from, my requirement, say it loud, "I won't be a product of my environment... we playing to win""— MEEK MILL (Mandela Freestyle)

GO LISTEN TO GREATNESS

My favorite artist by a long shot is Dreezy, The light skin Keith Sweat, The boy, Mr. OvO, or better known as Drake.
To me, Drake's music is amazing for too many reasons. So, my message is simply to go and listen to greatness if you are not familiar with him, and thank me later. (No pun intended.)

"Lately, I feel the haters eatin' away at my confidence. They scream out my failures and whisper my accomplishments." — DRAKE (6 pm in New York)

LOVE AND ACCEPT YOURSELF

J. Cole is my second favorite artist.
J. Cole opened up an amazing perspective on life that might have already been introduced to me before, but it

resonated the most when he rapped about it in his project, Forrest Hills Drive.

In the song "Love yours," J. Cole said, "Always going to be a bigger house somewhere but nigga feel me, long as the people in that motherfucker love you dearly, always going to be a whip that's better than the one you got, always gon' be some clothes fresher than the ones you rock, always gon' be a bitch that's badder out there on the tours but you ain't never gon' be happy until you love yours."

That rhyme is so deep and so well-articulated to me. He's suggesting that you could never obtain true happiness, which is the ultimate form of success (in my opinion) if you don't love yourself.

If your success is determined by anything other than who you are, you'll never be in control or feel truly successful. At the beginning of my book, I mentioned success as being subjective, and this is where I got that from.

Just like Cole, I heartily believe true happiness comes from accepting and loving yourself.

Now, just because you love and accept yourself does not mean you'll be happy all the time or that the struggles you face won't affect you. That is an absurd thought. Adopting this idea will simply make you more equipped to deal with your life.

Also, let it be clear I am not suggesting you don't attempt to have better things or encouraging no change for that matter. This book is all about changing for the better. Change is good and inevitable. However, do not trick yourself into believing you'll love yourself only after some change or certain accomplishments.

Putting conditions on when you're going to love yourself will make it nearly impossible to ever be happy with who you truly are because then you'll be training your mind to love your accomplishments as opposed to loving yourself.

"We ain't picture perfect but we worth the picture still." — J.COLE (Crooked Smile)

MAKE DECISIONS THAT MAKE SENSE TO YOU

Mr. West, Mr. West, Mr. Fresh, Mr. by-his-self-he-so-impressed, comes in third.

I can't vouch for everything that Kanye says, but if you listen to his music, you can tell he is undeniably a very smart human being.

Kanye's music reinforces my confidence and a mentality that makes sense to me. Hearing his songs inspired me to continue accomplishing goals (such as this book) without having to accumulate diploma after diploma.

My whole life, I was told by society that school is the way towards success and that your grades determine your intelligence, but I just about had it with that false narrative.

Going to college and seeing how some of these students with high grades are dumb as fuck in many aspects and not actually doing anything substantial with their lives made me realize that generalization was far from accurate. Of course, there is a good number of incredibly smart students that have exceptional grades, and are doing great things, but believing good grades is the most accurate way to measure intelligence and predict greatness is foolish.

One of the smartest decisions I ever made was dropping out of college. Not because I don't believe in education, but because in life, you have to learn how to make decisions that make sense to you, not the people around you. And the reason I was in college wasn't because it made sense to me, but the people around me.

"She so self-conscious, she has no idea what she doing in college. The major that she majored in don't make no money but she won't drop out her parents would look at her funny, now, tell me that ain't insecurr, the concept of school seems so securr" – KANYE WEST (All Falls Down)

USE COMPETITION TO FUEL YOUR AMBITION

Jay Z is my fourth favorite artist.

Wanting to relate to some of Jay Z's lyrics continues to influence me to work—not only harder, but smarter.

Comparing your success with others can come off as shallow, but it depends on how you look at it. If you're accomplishing your goals ethically (meaning you're not screwing somebody over to accomplish them), it is okay to look at it as a sport.

Jay Z is a little arrogant in his raps, but so was Michael Jordan when playing ball. Everyone who is an athlete understands that is part of what makes sports so entertaining. Shit talking and trying to prove you are the best or better than others on the field elevates competition.

Jay Z got a freestyle where he said, "Quit playing childish games with a grown man, I don't give a fuck about cars or chrome rims, I got apartments you can put your home in." Although that sounds arrogant, I love the mentality behind it, and to me, it's inspiring.

I'm not interested in owning chrome rims or nice cars over real estate or appreciating assets, and one day I will own apartments that are big as some houses.

I hope this section inspires people to hustle harder, especially if you are around me, because the better the competition around me, the better I will become. And I will rather be the worse player in the NBA than the best player in just my neighborhood.

"I should probably copyright this I promise they ain't gonna like this." — JAY Z (I Got the Keys)

Do not allow others to dictate the person you're going to be

Speaking of influence, too many people live life scared of being their authentic self because of others.

I consider myself a very confident person, but it doesn't mean I don't get shy or insecure. I was actually considered a quiet person by my family for a very long time.

I never liked being quiet. I was just afraid to voice my opinion because whenever I tried to say something, everybody would say, "Oh, he does talk" or, "I thought he didn't talk," and that would shut me down immediately.

My family from my dad's side were unapologetic comedians, so whenever I said something that didn't live up to the hype THEY would build up, they would say things like, "Damn, you never talk, and that's all you had to say" then get back to their loud conversations.

If you are somebody who is quiet only because you have been conditioned to be quiet; you better start talking! Most of your aunts and uncles aren't saying meaningful shit anyway. Yeah, you're going to bomb a joke or two, maybe even a thousand if you're not funny. Sometimes you will say things that nobody cares about, but so what? Most people do. Why do you not feel worthy of such privilege?

If talking and voicing your opinion is important to you, then do it, or you will constantly continue to allow others to dictate who you're going to be.

Yes, coming out of your comfort zone could be hard, but life gets so much better when you don't restrict yourself from being who you truly are because of the judgment of others.

I had to take some heat from my family to dismiss that title of being 'the quiet kid,' and it was a challenge. I still bomb jokes and say dumb things very often, but it's worth it because talking and voicing my opinion is important to me; it brings me true joy.

Allow yourself to feel

Family will always have good and negative things to add to your life. It is okay to reflect on the negatives and attempt to get rid of them.

I grew up in a culture where crying wasn't all that acceptable, especially as a male.

My dad's side of the family is your stereotypical Mexican family. They love joking around by poking fun of each other, and if you're somebody emotional, they will have a field day with you because being sensitive is not tolerated.

If you ever showed signs of wanting to cry for not a good enough reason (aside from death, most reasons were not good enough reasons to cry in front of the family), you'd get the classic, "*Quiere llorar, quiere llorar…*" chant by everybody, which translates into "He/she wants to cry" hoping you'd cry and if you did, that shit was so funny to everybody (adults included). If you had nice parents, they might coddle you after, usually the mom, but most will tell you to suck it up and not take it so serious.

I love that side of our culture that teases and plays around all the time because it teaches us not to take anything too personal, but it definitely has its negative side.

Aside from my breakups, the last two times I remember crying without being intoxicated were when I saw my aunt in her casket and when a friend of mine got murdered.

Usually, I could control my crying, but when I saw my aunt just lying there, I couldn't, and it felt good to let the tears fall with no intoxication attached to them. Still, I felt ashamed because there were people around watching.

In a space where it is totally acceptable to cry, I still felt embarrassed and weak.

When they told me that my friend Luis passed, it hurt me for many reasons: thinking about how his family must have felt, how the odds of that happening to my brother over him were much higher, and because he was so young and talented.

Growing up, Luis would often compliment me about how well I played soccer or acknowledge a funny joke I said. Those comments really helped my confidence and self-esteem because he was somebody with an energy that was felt as soon as he walked into the room. Out of the generation of people I grew up around, he was definitely the smartest and funniest, in my opinion. Since I've always valued intelligence, in a way, I looked up to him when I was a teen.

Thinking about all that really hurt my heart, and it still does whenever I think of him.

The day I heard the news, I felt like crying, and a little voice inside of me kept telling me to hold it in, but I'm glad I didn't listen to it because it felt really good to let that hurt out.

Being conditioned to feel ashamed for crying has forced me to bottle up my emotions too many times, and bottling up my pain has always resulted in anger and aggressive behavior where there was no need for it.

Too many times, I've passed judgment on others who cry about things I would never cry about because I have convinced myself subconsciously that such emotions are absurd.

This is not a healthy mentality to adopt, and even though it has been a slow process for me, I'm glad I'm beginning to shift away from it.

We need to allow ourselves more often to just "feel" without feeling ashamed.

It is okay to cry if you're hurting, we all have emotions, and sometimes is necessary to let them out before they begin eating away at us.

Accept your reality

Allowing yourself to feel does not only apply to feeling sad but being happy.

When I think back to the happiest time in my life, I go back to my sophomore year of high school. I was dating a junior named Vanessa (number 10 from the volleyball game on page 3). She had a white complexion, very pretty honey/amber-colored eyes, and a pretty smile. There is this one memory I still have that takes me back to that time, and it's simply of us walking down the hall after class, holding hands and smiling at one another.

This was the happiest time of my life, not because I was in love with Vanessa—I had yet to experience true love—but because I felt so innocent and free of any worry that actually mattered.

After 2016, I was unhappy for about four years due to the worry clouding my judgment. Even in the best of moments, my mind would drift into its own imagination of how much better life could be if only I didn't have any problems to worry about.

I would often tell myself, "Man, if only I didn't have such and such problems to worry about, life would be great right now." Except a lot of moments were great in life around that time, I was just not allowing myself to savor them. In my twisted head, resisting felt "better" because there was some guilt to enjoying myself if it wasn't the happiness I kept picturing in my head.

I refuse to look at life like that anymore.

Somewhere in 2019, I realized I had to stop thinking like that after my brother had gotten himself in a situation that put him in jail.

When this happened, my life felt surreal. I had nightmares and trouble sleeping for a few months because I couldn't believe my little brother was behind bars and could possibly be there for many years.

This moment felt like life punching in my mouth really hard, forcing me to stop imagining what life could be and making me deal with what it actually was.

Happiness is mental, and as hard as it might be, you have to discipline your mind into it.

Many factors might determine your happiness, and because you are unique in certain ways, what works for me might not necessarily work for you. But being both humans, you and I might be more alike than you think. So, what works for me might very well work for you, too, with a little bit of optimism.

Working on accepting your reality and keeping focus on your blessings instead of your misfortunes will go a long way.

There is nothing wrong with missing, reminiscing, wanting better, hoping for better, and working for better. However, don't miss out on enjoying your current blessings because you're waiting on something that might not ever come or that is no longer there.

Although life has been tough on me, it also has been quite beautiful. There is and has been so much good in it, and I'm very glad it didn't take me forever to realize I have to enjoy it all before it again becomes just a memory.

For me to wait for that same feeling I had in sophomore year is silly because it's past. I will never be fifteen or sixteen years old, with a pure careless mind and a pretty upper classman as a girlfriend, experiencing all these cool new emotions. I also can't control who people decide to become or the choices they choose to make. I could only control the decisions I make and how I choose to look at my reality.

My parents are still alive, and I have to enjoy that. Someday my reality will be that they're not, and I still have to find happiness then. I could be gone before them for all I know, and I wouldn't want them to stop looking for happiness even then.

My aunt passed before her parents did, and the healthiest thing my grandparents could do was accept that reality. I could never pretend to know what it feels like to lose a daughter, but if my grandparents consider their sons and daughter a blessing, they got three more to enjoy.

Don't wait for your parents to change their flaws to enjoy them

My mother is not the best listener, and that's what would stand out the most to me about her for a long time. This often caused me to argue with her because I felt like she didn't care to understand me. It wasn't until a couple of years back when I realized that not just my mother but my parents don't owe me anything, and they won't be here forever.

Society often tells us our parent's jobs are to vend over backward for us, simply because they had us. If anything goes wrong, they're the ones to blame for our shortcomings. It is not always true in my reckoning, and that's a very ungrateful way of thinking.

At what point do we ever blame ourselves for being shitty sons and daughters? As a son or daughter, how often do we try to understand our parents? How hard do we actually try to build a relationship with our parents? How often do we ask them about their day? How much do we actually know about them besides their birthdays? What is really important to them? How was their childhood? What is, or was the relationship between their parents and them?

What traumas do they have? What have you done for them to deserve what you believe you deserve from them?

So often, we try to build relationships with strangers, but not when it comes to our own parents. We hold their flaws against them because we forget they're regular human beings.

We should accept our parents and love them, not like we do strangers every day, but much more. A huge majority of our parents really do the best they can, and we only focus on what they do wrong because we feel entitled to their love, affection, and what they can provide to us.

As a last message to this chapter, I would like to beg you not to wait for your parents to change their flaws to enjoy them; you might miss out on their beauty. And if you no longer got your parents, enjoy those who genuinely love you, in spite of their imperfections.

SIDE NOTE: If you have parents that are really toxic to you, then ignore this section. Of course, some parents fail to do basic things for their children, but this section is intended to help daughters/sons reflect on how much they actually contribute to the relationship they have with their parents.

Often, most of our parents did not have the same head start in life as us, and we forget we owe that to THEM. I know, it's hard to recognize that because it's easier to feel entitled and not accept we are often worst sons/daughters than they are parents, but this could be a sign to change that behavior!

Dear Mom,

A man is only as strong as the women in his life. Mom, you've been strong for so long for our family. I admire you almost as much as I love you. You always made me understand by explaining things to me as if I was intelligent enough to understand. You have reinforced all the positive aspects in me and pointed out all the negative ones as well, helping me avoid being arrogant but confident as one can be. Because of you, I know how to walk, talk, throw, juggle a soccer ball, catch with a baseball mitt, batt with proper form, and most importantly, the reason why I can see the good in others. I am short of words to describe how much you mean to me and how much you've brought to the table. Still, I will always be man enough to pay tribute to you in real life, not just with words but showing actions and standing as tall as you need me to stand. You are forever beautiful to me: physically and mentally. I love you, ma, and will always love you with all my heart.

Enlightenments part two

You're entitled to be subjective about things in your life, but it's better to be objective when you're trying to learn something new

Religion is an interesting topic to me, but it is also quite a controversial one for many people. Our beliefs are susceptible to our emotions — we protect them at all costs, and everyone is entitled to feel how they feel about what they believe in. But if we could get past our emotions and biases, maybe we can learn a lot from one another.

When people have a conversation about such a delicate topic for understanding as opposed to debate is a wonderful thing — we become united for the first time.

You will never meet anybody who thinks just like you. It does not matter if you're of the same race, religion, gender, or even the same family. What you will meet for sure are people who think nothing like you, and you will still be forced to interact with one another daily.

In the following writing, I will share my perspective on the moralities of the religion I was born into, Catholicism.

Whether you're Catholic, of a different religion, atheist, etc., I beg you to read the rest of my content with an open mind to allow yourself to learn something new.

FRANCISCO GALLARDO

Definition of Catholicism according to Cambridge Dictionary: the beliefs and activities of the Roman Catholic Church.

The Catholic Religion has seven sacraments: Baptism, Confirmation, Eucharist, Penance, Anointing of the ill, Marriage, and Ordination.

These sacraments are religious ceremonies/rituals performed through Catholicism.

The following section is a simplified explanation of these rituals based on my knowledge and experience.

I was baptized a Catholic.

Baptism is the act in which you have "holy" water poured on your head by a priest at a church to announce you are a "child of God" and member of the catholic religion. For the most part, this is done during your infancy because your parents decided you should be baptized — that's when I got baptized. (I know that because I've seen photos of me crying as I'm being passed among my parents and godparents during this ritual.)

Godparents are a couple your parents decide will be assigned at each of these rituals to be your "spiritual role models."

Later, still during my infancy, I did my confirmation.

During confirmation, you simply confirm (your parents actually) you're still a "child of God" and accept the Catholic religion through a ceremony at church.

During my middle childhood, I did my first communion.

A first communion is when you receive the Eucharist for the first time. This requires preparation through catechism to learn the core values of the catholic religion. I will not get into all the details of the Eucharist to avoid shifting away from the actual point, but the idea is the commemoration of the last super during Mass.

According to Catholicism, the last super is the final meal Jesus Christ prepared for his apostles in Jerusalem before his crucifixion.

Jesus Christ is the Son of God who was sent to earth from heaven to die for our sins many years back according to Catholicism.

Mass is a celebration amongst Catholics where "God" is worshipped at a Church.

The people that attend Mass and have done their first communion may receive the Communion wafer and a sip of wine at a particular time during Mass.

A "Communion wafer" is pretty much a thin round wafer that is used to represent the body of Christ, and the wine is used to represent his blood. You are only worthy of lining up to consume the body (wafer) and blood (wine) of Chris if you have confessed.

Confession or penance is the practice of telling a priest all your wrongdoings or sins. When described, the word *penance* is usually thought of as self-punishment, but the catholic religion uses it under a different context. When you have confessed your sins to a priest, he absolves you from those sins "through God" and tells you to do certain prayers as your penance.

The idea of the anointing of the ill is to help the sick by strengthening their mind, body, and soul. Priests mostly do this one, and it is not, or at least it was not as heavily persuaded to pursuit compared to every other sacrament in all of my time involved with the Church.

Matrimony, most commonly referred to as marriage, is a commitment in which you devote yourself to a partner of your choice (as long as it is not the same sex) through all good and bad, till death do you apart. A mass is celebrated as part of this ritual. During this mass/ritual, a priest (usually) is the one to unify the two of you in the name of the Father, the Son, and the Holy Spirit.

Holy order is the process in which men are ordained to become priests. There is more to this sacrament, but that is the main idea of it.

Now that you have a basic understanding of the sacraments of this religion, I want to touch up on certain things.

As I've gotten older, I can tell you better about my beliefs, but do not focus on what I believe to be true or not, focus on how you can use any information I'll share to your advantage.

I do not commit to believing every aspect of any religion, even the religion I confirmed to be a part of. Still, I am open to learning from any religion if the teachings make any sense.

The catholic religion has many good things to learn from, such as the sacraments I just explained. But just like a lot of good teachings from other religions, these teachings are often overlooked. This usually happens because we don't understand the teachings, we misinterpret them, we are not interested enough to learn about them, or simply because we don't know how to utilize their good doctrines.

I had no choice when it came to my baptism—I was an infant. For all I know, the real reason why I was crying in my photos is because I wasn't born into Islam.

When I "confirmed" I indeed wanted to be part of the catholic religion, same thing—my brain was still not capable of making sound decisions. You would think pouting and crying while being at mass was my way of expressing I didn't want to be there.

I do not believe to be a son of God simply because of the religion I was born into. I do, however, believe there is a God, and I am one of his creations.

I do not believe in every aspect of the Eucharist, but I believe confessing your wrongdoings can help you liberate your mind.

When I speak to my spiritual guider Father Bobby (a priest and the second greatest human being I have encounter after my father) and open up about what I feel guilt for, shame, sadness, etc., he gives me sound advice. Whether it's through confession or not, I feel a little more mentally stable after our conversations.

You don't have to be baptized a Catholic to practice that; talking to a psychologist has a parallel purpose.

I choose not to dismiss the idea of confession just because I don't believe everything I was taught about it to be the truth.

Even though I have not specifically practiced anointing the ill, I really believe to be blessed with the ability to help others, and part of that is why I'm writing this. The ill isn't just older folks who are about to die. Some people feel dead inside dealing with their struggles in life. I have stuff I deal with and have dealt with, as you can tell, yet, it makes me feel alive to spark others to do the same.

Helping others without expecting something in return can really bring you great satisfaction, and if everybody thought this way, this world would be so much better.

I want to marry someday when I find the woman that is meant to be with me. The idea of devoting yourself to just one person seems absurd to certain people, but that's what I want. Committing to experience life with a partner I'm truly in love with sounds beautiful to me.

I would love for father Bobby to be the priest who celebrates mass during that day. Still, if I'm excommunicated because my beliefs are no longer aligned with his or any other priest, the most important thing for me will be to be a good partner to the love of my life.

Today I differ spiritually from religion which I was not able to do at a young age. It is hard to do because they're very much intertwined, and religion often limits objectivity when it comes to right and wrong.

For example, there is a lot of flaw from my perspective on those sacraments I just explained, but there is also so much good you can get out of them if you're not forced or bullied to be an extremist about the practices. This often happens with catholic folks — they go from devoting themselves to these religious practices to dismissing all they've ever learned because they don't agree with all of the teachings. It is often a priest or parent's rhetoric that either bullies them to believe everything they are taught to be accurate or everything they have learned to be inaccurate.

I chose not to be bullied in or out and rather objectively look at information to see if it makes any sense.

I strongly believe in God, but my intention with the following writing isn't to start a debate on who God is, what he looks like, who he should be to you, or why you should believe there is even a God. We get nothing out of that but a battle of ego. I intend to get past that debate and simply offer my information and point of view, hoping it can help you in any way.

SIDE NOTE: Early in my life I learned about the Ten Commandments taught in Catholicism. Later on I read about the Ten Commandments taught by Protestants. When I compared these commandments, the morality of them were indistinguishable to me (which makes sense, since they both derived from Christian values), but their phrasing is slightly different, and I understand this must be pointed out.

Please understand if you are Catholic or a Protestant that my intention isn't to preach that these are THE commandments people should follow — they are the commandments I follow, and how I understand them.

I live by the following moralities to have a better life, not to avoid being condemned. I use the following information not to be a good religious folk but to keep track in being a good human being and son of God.

COMMANDMENTS

I am the Lord your God: you should not have any strange Gods before me

The idea of what a "strange God" is, or what righteous moralities are, could be challenged because you can always argue it comes down to subjectivity, but if you're a logical person, it's just really not that deep.

Morals that will lead you to harm yourself or others are simply not righteous, and a God who wants you to harm yourself or others is a strange God.

You should not make idols

This commandment states not to make idols, but the root of it is idolization in general.

IDOLIZATION OF LEADERS:

This world needs leaders to continue to evolve, and we have been fortunate to have had a lot of great ones. Martin Luther King Jr., for example, was a great activist who brought people together and fought against an oppressive system.

Nonetheless, though, all leaders must be audited, and the best way to do so is to go back to the first commandment and ask if what we are supporting is righteous. If any leader is asking you to harm yourself or others, you might be fighting for the wrong shit.

Adolf Hitler was a dictator who convinced others that Jews were the inferior class, and therefore they should be murdered. (Holocaust 1941).

To a lot of people that sounds crazy, but this was possible because a lot of people also believed it wasn't, and they were actually doing right by it.

IDOLIZATION OF RELIGION:

Technically, all scriptures on earth were created by humans, but I most certainly believe a huge amount of the information in them was written by God through humans.

However, because humans are flawed, not everything written in the scriptures is precise, and not everything that is written precisely is interpreted correctly.

There is nothing wrong with religious practices. A lot of what I'm writing pertains to religious practices, but idolizing a religion can make you susceptible to manipulation by flawed humans through the use of "God's will."

You should not take the name of the Lord your God in vein

This commandment is much related to the first two, and YOUR understanding plays a huge role in its virtue.

To preach very assertive as to what God wants because you feel you understand God's will can be beneficial and also very dangerous.

Although I believe many priests to have a high level of intellect and pure intention when it comes to their preaching, I also believe them to be the most naïve when it comes to the understanding of these first three commandments because they don't understand their logic is not farfetched from a terrorist's.

When terrorists do an inhumane act in the name of a God, it is not right. Whether you believe in God or not, to murder innocent people is wrong. It doesn't matter what your religion is. But to somebody who truly believes their God wanted that, they don't see anything wrong with it, and they actually feel they are honorable, just like when devoted religious folks (priests, for example) discriminate towards somebodies sexual preference, race, or religion based on THEIR understanding of scriptures or God.

Remember to keep holy the Lord's day

In Christianity, Sunday is the day to worship the Lord God, enjoy your family and the fruits of your labor.

Family will forever be one of the most important things on my agenda, no matter what. When my family is good and I'm good with my family, I am the healthiest I can be.

There is nothing wrong with being ambitious, especially if you don't come from wealth (you can read about this in section Sloth-Greed on pages 98-104), but if you can't give yourself at least one day out of the week to enjoy yourself and your family, you are a slave to your ambition.

Whether you believe or not in going to church, or taking Sunday off, making it a habit to rest one day of the week and make time for those you love will really improve your overall well-being.

Honor your father and your mother

Having a father and a mother is like having a strong foundation in life.

If your parents are alive, honoring them will bring you strong peace of mind.

I tempt to believe I have the best parents anybody can ask for, and if you feel the same, I am thrilled because then, just like me, you have had a head start on the level of difficulty this life can bring. Now make sure to show your gratitude for it!

If it weren't for my parents, I would not be here, and if it weren't for how they raised me, navigating through life would be so much harder. I am eternally grateful for them, and honoring them in every way possible will forever fulfill my heart.

Understandably, not all parents are great parents, and some really don't deserve your gratitude, but if you had bad parents, do your kids better and teach them about this principle.

If we were all to follow this commandment, it would be a beautiful cycle: your parents doing right by your grandparents, you doing right by your parents, and your kids doing right by you.

You should not commit adultery

This commandment states not to commit adultery, but the morality is simply not to cheat.

You don't need to be married to take your exclusive relationship seriously. Marriage can complicate a situation a lot more, but the action will hurt the same if the emotions are genuine.

I have been "good" at staying faithful in my serious relationships because I've always understood cheating to be wrong, but I had a slip up in my last relationship. I know a lot of women are reading this thinking, "Uh, uh, there is no such thing as a slip up, you're a fuck boy!" (Fuck boy is referred to as a male who doesn't respect/appreciate women.) And sure, it is fair to refer to me as a fuck boy for cheating, but that mistake helped me understand why males cheat even if they are deeply in love with one person.

While still dating Nina, I went to a party by myself, and there I met an attractive girl whom I clicked with off the bat.

As the night went on, we kept right by each other. Aside from her laughing at my jokes, she kept boosting my self-esteem. One thing I remember her repeating to me was, "You're cute and funny; your girlfriend fucked up for letting you come to this party by yourself. "

In my head, the more I heard this, the more I convinced myself it was okay to lean into the pleasure of how her compliments made me feel.

As the night went on, I began to tell myself, "This girl is right. Nina did fuck up for letting me show up here alone because I'm that motherfucking guy!"

I did not have sex with this girl because I really did feel bad after making out with her, but I sure wanted to.

This girl's interest made me feel so good and valuable. It wasn't all about the physical attraction I felt for her, but the feeling of an attractive woman showing so much interest in me.

The ironic part about that experience, though, is that my ego got stroke for a night, but my security deflated after for the rest of the relationship.

Although Nina never showed suspicion of ever cheating on me in return, after that night, I began doubting what she was doing whenever I wasn't with her. In my mind, I often felt like it was just a matter of time before Karma got me back, and that guilt is just not worth it at all.

Infidelity is wrong for a male and a female, but I can't speak from a women's perspective about why they do it.

However, as a male who has cheated and has been around many other males who cheat or have cheated (about 99% of the guys I've ever met), I can better explain why most of us do it. And of course, I'm not saying every male feels or thinks exactly the same, but similar, and so hopefully, we can change after understanding ourselves a little better.

One reason as to why men cheat is lust. (If you want a deeper dive on this, turn to the section about Lust on page 109)

Lust is a hard emotion to keep under control, and instinctively most of us men want to have sex with every physically attractive woman we see, no matter her personality.

Another reason, and the most prevalent, in my opinion, is conditioning.

Society has trained us, males, to measure our worth based on how much attention we receive from women.

As men, we feel proud when we can sleep with many women because it is not easy to get their attention unless we have something to show for, and aside from sex feeling great, the expression of lust is a safe way to confirm somebody's interest. This often causes men to subconsciously correlate a women's sexual interest in them to how much they're really worth.

Whether you do it consciously or subconsciously, measuring your value based on a woman's interest in you is unhealthy. It is not healthy because, just like with a drug, when you get it, you'll get a feeling of instant gratification that will never be fulfilling. It will affect you internally, leading you to unhealthy relationships.

Cheating will never be fulfilling, and as corny as it might sound, it is just not worth it, or needed, when you learn to love yourself and your partner.

SIDE NOTE: I've met so many guys that brag about cheating on their significant others, and you all need to understand your woman is a reflection of you. If you think your woman is stupid enough to never find out about your affairs, chances are people think you're stupid too—you chose each other for a reason.

Men are constantly trying to prove loyalty and seek loyalty. I always hear guys talk about how real they are and how they give it up, etc., which is cool. People should aspire to be loyal, but why are men so invested in being loyal to other men and not their women?

Men fail to be loyal to their women all the time and are nowhere near ashamed as to when they fail their men.

Men will kill a stranger to prove to a stranger their loyalty and worth but won't even attempt to be loyal to the woman they love. Hu? What kind of backward logic is that?

You should not steal

In the United States, we live in a society where most of us work to get what we want. We exchange something that belongs to us in return for something that doesn't.

If we all just took what we didn't work for, we would not be able to live in a functional society.

If you live in America, it is obvious that not everybody has the same privileges and opportunities. Your skin, nationality, gender, age, and maybe other things could make it difficult to get ahead in life. There is still no justification as to why you should steal for a living.

I've heard people say they only stole because of their circumstances — that they needed to feed their babies, make ends meet, etc. And those are good excuses, but fuck all that.

Why are you in a situation where you can't feed your baby and get a job?

My parents have three kids. My mother drove all of us to school in a scooter-type bike when we lived in Mexico to save gas and not spend on a car. She cooked food that would last us for multiple meals. My father took risks to come into the United States and got plenty of jobs while not knowing any English. Mannn, fuck your excuses, figure it out!

It frustrates me when people have loser mentalities because there are a hundred excuses for why you're not doing what you should be doing.

Do not take what does not belong to you! It's that simple.

There is always somebody whose head works a million miles per minute (mine sometimes) and comes up with responses like, "technically, nobody owns anything, who really decided you can even own land, to begin with? Land should be everybody's." My response to that is, "I'm writing a self-development book, not the constitution."

Learn how to crawl before you can walk.

It would be great to live in a world where everything was 100% fair from the beginning of time, and we all got the same start out of the womb, but unfortunately, it's not that way, but fortunately, there is always room for progress, and the best progress starts within you.

This world would be better, and you would be a better person if you decided not to take what did not belong to you; it's that easy.

You should not bear false witness (Lie)

This commandment does not only mean to not lie about what somebody did, but not to state something about somebody because of their sex, beliefs, color, preferences, associations, or what you heard about them. Those things do not say enough about a person to state anything concrete about who they really are.

Defamation of character is ugly and very dangerous, and we have to stop talking "through God" to excuse such behavior.

When I was younger, there was a point in my life when I thought there were catholic people and atheists, and the atheist people were the bad people.

As I got older, I came to find out there were other religions, and that not all catholic people were good people, just like not all atheists or people who belonged to other religions were bad.

When my brother started hanging out with the neighborhood's gang, I heard so much chitter chat about our family from religious folks that lived in our area, especially older women who constantly prayed to show how devoted they were to their religion.

One time my mother went to church and she told me how a priest started preaching down about this lady whose kid was "no good." His preaching consisted of him clowning the lady's parenting based on how the kid turned out. I had heard him express similar rhetoric before during mass but never thought anything of it, until it hit home.

I don't care about the title of any human being, any person who believes is okay to judge a mother who they don't live with, and while having no actual experience in parenting or giving birth themselves, is wrong.

I know my mother like the palm of my hand so I know she, too, to some extent, felt like she had failed my brother as a mother, but she will always be wrong to feel that way.

I've witnessed my parents' parenting very closely with my brother, sister, and me. Our fuck ups should not reflect their parenting as they did an exceptional job. You can get this review not just from me, but from my brother and sister, which is the actual source, and not gossip or what the fuck people want to believe.

Father,

I hope you read this someday to obtain more wisdom and become a better man of God. This lady's son is dead, and I want to let you know that some people who judged my mother's parenting probably did it because your voice is so powerful. Those people believed your false testimony towards that mother's parenting, so they thought it was acceptable to judge another mother like mine. You are not courageous for speaking such inaccurate statements in a blunt/passionate way.

The main point of this section isn't to talk down about the priest or imply he is a bad person (He isn't, I've met him, but people with that much power should be audited)—I'm sharing this to let mothers know that priests are not always right. They're actually often wrong when it comes to judging people who do not share their same beliefs. Deep inside, you mothers know how much you have worked to see YOUR children prosper, so do not let other people take that away from you, not even these "holy" folks.

Most of my friends are Catholics, and they are great people. I also have friends from other religions/races (and I don't mean I know or tolerate working with some people from other races/religions, so I use that relationship before saying some inappropriate shit about that race/religion to not seem like a bad person)—I mean, I actually hang out with these people because I like them. I have all kinds of different friends because, to me, they are dope people, and I did not judge them based on anything other than personal interaction.

Bearing false witness and spreading gossip does not make you a good person, no matter how devoted you are to your Hail Mary's or how passionate and accurate you are at regurgitating religious quotes.

Learn how to lead with love and spread love, no matter somebody's sex, race, or religious beliefs. That is what ultimately brings us all together and makes us better sons/daughters of God.

You should not covet

If you live in America, you have incredible freedom.

Yes, there is bias, prejudice, racism, sexism, etc., but there is an opportunity for almost anything you set your mind to.

You want to get rich? There are ways. You want to be with a beautiful woman? No law says you can't attempt to go after as many beautiful women as you want until you get one.

Knowing this should make you want to stay the fuck out of anything that got nothing to do with you.

Live and enjoy everything you have in YOUR life, and you will be happier that way. Count your own blessing and be thankful for them instead of yearning for somebody else's.

Also, I know I talked about cheating and how you should resist it if you love your partner. But you should also resist yourself from going after people that are in relationships.

Do not be the reason for creating drama in a household or your friend's life. Those are not traits of an honorable person.

We're human, so we aren't just going to be attracted to who we fall in love with, no matter how much we love that person. And yes, we should be accountable if we cheat, and it's our responsibility if we fuck up, but if you're single, go and persuade somebody else, or you're wrong too. There are millions of people out there who are single and ready to mingle, just like you!

Some people are very good at talking, flirting, and convincing people to make wrong decisions, and even the nicest people could be charm for the worse. But you will be a better person if you're not the reason a good marriage or relationship becomes toxic.

I know being the person to charm and convince somebody nice to slip up can stroke your ego, but ego strokes will never be fulfilling — ever.

DEADLY SINS

In the catholic religion, there are seven deadly sins: wrath, sloth, greed, pride, envy, lust and gluttony. The idea of these sins is that we all have these emotions, and when we don't get a grip of them or keep them in check, they will consume us and make our lives a living hell.

Don't feel bad if you experience these feelings; we all feel them. But do feel bad if you don't work on disciplining such emotions.

You should not murder / WRATH

This commandment and deadly sin just had to go together for me to explain their dangers better.

Imagine a world where there were no murders. We are all going to die, that is inevitable. Murder is not inevitable. In this world, it might seem like it is, but it's not. You can choose not to take part in it.

I'm ashamed to admit that at some point in my life, I was waiting on the day I had to murder. My intrusive thoughts came from being hurt and angry. Today, I no longer feel this way, and I'm really proud of myself for working on dismissing such thoughts and emotions.

It is very common to hear about people you know dying in Chicago. Too many young souls get murdered every day. Many times a minority murders another minority, and sometimes even the people who are supposed to "protect" us fail on purpose and abuse their power.

Two years ago, I thought about my brother dying often and how it would be a nasty sight for many people, including myself if that ever happened, but in my head, I was "ready" for that sight.

I thought of my brother dying as a game over—a sign that God didn't exist and he wasn't really looking over me. I was ready to throw my values and morals out the window due to my rage.

How hypocritical of me to accept God gave us free will and the guide to living a better life, yet, I expected Him to stop other people's free will because I believed in Him.

One day, as I was getting home from work, my father received a call. I saw his face turn pale and full of worry as he handed the phone to me to translate. Right away, I felt negative energy entering my body. The call was from the hospital. As soon as I heard the lady say she was calling from the hospital, my heartbeat started rising because I realized my brother wasn't home, and my first thought was that something had happened to him. The call, sure enough, was about him. And after confirming it was my brother they had at the hospital, the lady said she couldn't disclose further information other than he was bruised up and sedated at the moment.

Once I wrote the hospital's address, I hung the phone up and drove my parents to the hospital that night because I could tell they were in no state of mind to drive anywhere.

I was anxious myself, but moments like this are what shape you as a man. I had to pretend I was fine the whole way there for my mother and father. I had to be ready for anything because I could see in their faces that they weren't.

When we got there and were able to see him, you could see through the small thin robe he had on, bruises on all parts of his body, a swollen lip, and almost a distorted face. They later told us his jaw was dislocated. The doctor explained the cops found him in the street intoxicated, and as he tried to run away, he fell flat on his face more than once, and that's how the injuries happened. He said when the paramedics came, he was extremely aggressive, so they had to tie him down and use sedatives to calm him down.

When I heard the story the first time, I thought, "Bullshit, those pussy ass cops probably beat him," and my whole body began to feel hot. As I felt my anger increasing, my instinct told me to yell at this doctor and intimidate him into telling me the truth. Even then, if he said the same thing, he was lying, and I should choke him until he told me the truth. But when I glanced at my parents, my brain told me to calm down because my parents didn't need anything else on top of what was already going on.

That moment felt just like when in cartoons, you have an angel on one ear and a devil on the other, pressuring to make a decision. Except the voices were my emotions and my intelligence, not an angel or a devil.

Good men are supposed to put their selfishness aside in moments like this for the people they claim to care about. It's easier to blame people like some cops or persons from a gang when you got love for somebody, and sometimes it's really not your loved one's fault, and they do get screwed over unfairly, but my brother could have avoided that night.

My brother could have avoided a lot in his life by making better decisions, but he isn't the only one. We all could prevent a lot if we can learn from our mistakes.

Taking accountability is hard, but it is part of becoming a better person.

I was at the hospital all night that day, and there I decided I was done fighting shadows. I'm not perfect by any means, so I'm bound to keep making mistakes, but seeing clear helps a whole lot.

Not fighting shadows was a great decision for me. For a long time, I was angry and directed it randomly. My thought process was: if God doesn't take care of my family, then it's fuck everybody. Nobody will mess with me; watch how I prove everybody is pussy compared to me if something happens to my little brother.

I was wrong to think that way. God gave us free will and blueprints on how to live a good life, but if people refuse to take accountability and choose to resent God and other people instead, it becomes harder. It's like taking your anger out by punching a wall.

Smart people don't cut their noses to spite their faces.

Part of me is relieved that my relationship with my brother became shaky around that time because I'm convinced I would have ended up dead or in jail. My brother blocking me out of whatever he had going on with himself was good in a way because most nights those two years, I was very uneasy and battling with negative thoughts. Those thoughts made it easier for me to be vulnerable and susceptible to fucking up. Had my brother been comfortable enough to open up to me and give me the green light on a name, any name, that name would be in a Facebook bio guaranteed. My life would also be hell on earth due to a decision like that. I thank God that today my life is closer to heaven on earth due to better decisions.

When you murder somebody, you hurt their loved ones, and that doesn't bring your loved ones back from the dead—you also hurt your loved ones, and if that brings fulfillment to you, then you're a wicked soul.

I have never murdered, but I sure was "mentality prepared" to do so due to wrath. And if I had done it, all I would have today is regret, more anxiety, and emptiness in my heart.

SLOTH

This emotion can be experienced by both genders (obviously), and women shouldn't be lazy either, but I could best deliver something substantial giving my perspective as a male.

To me, it will always be a man's job to protect and provide. Real men have to work hard—they can't afford to be lazy.

Women should be allowed to work whatever job they choose, but I'm happy my mother never had to work a job where she had to endure physical pain. She's five feet six inches and probably weighs no more than 125 pounds. My father worked many tough jobs his whole life to keep food on the table and prevent my mother from having to. He is five feet eight inches and weighs about 220 pounds. I would respect my father less if it was my mother who worked those physical jobs while he had such physique.

If you cannot provide basic necessities for your family because you're lazy, you've failed as a man. It is understandable that "protect and provide" is a vague way to describe a good man. I also understand some circumstances sometimes don't allow us to meet our duties despite sincere efforts. You could be born with certain disabilities, or you may have met an accident that limits your movement. In such circumstances which are beyond your control, it is not your fault.

But, when you have the ability and choice to protect and provide for your family, and you choose not to, due to your sloth, you become less of a man.

I want to be clear that I am not advocating that women should stay at home and be housewives, or that men shouldn't do chores, or that you should be embarrassed if your wife makes more money than you. Having a hard-working woman is such a beautiful thing. My mother is a very hard-working women, and my future wife has to be ambitious just like me. What I am saying is, as a man, you should always feel like that responsibility falls on you at the end of the day. And you should try your best to make sure your woman never ends in bad or uncomfortable situations.

I have worked many jobs, and there is a reason why males mostly do certain jobs. For example, I washed dishes for less than a year at the restaurant where my dad works, and it used to beat my ass. Rapidly taking food off plates, cups, and pans then carrying them to the kitchen is not the kind of job a lady should resort to in an attempt to make ends meet at home. I'm 175 pounds with a muscular body, rough hands, and I would still come home with my body hurting and my fingers looking like old folks from all that water.

I do not believe women aren't capable of doing this job or shouldn't be allowed to do this job, but a good man should put their woman in a position where she doesn't have to resort to such a painful job to stay afloat.

My future wife should never feel like she has to work any extreme physical job as long as I'm mobile.

It's understandable that even if you bust your ass, it still might not be enough to keep your wife from working tough jobs due to bad circumstances. But that's why just getting by in life is tricky because life is not as easy as just providing basic necessities.

How can you be a male and feel proud to send your daughter to school with some beat-up shoes or shabby clothes? How can you take pride in calling yourself a man while borrowing money instead of picking up extra shifts? Do you think your woman feels proud that you prefer to borrow money from other men instead of going to get it?

Asking for help shouldn't be embarrassing when you are going through tough times. We should help each other! But I'm talking about those who prefer to sit and watch a game and drink a beer when they know they have not set their family up right.

Of course, quality time with family matters, but that's why being good with money is so important. Most people like to say that time is money, but to me, money is time. The sooner you grasp the importance of money, the better. Not because money is happiness, but because it will make life easier for you and your family. It will afford you opportunities to spend leisure time with your loved ones without leaving them underprivileged.

Just getting by in life is okay, but be careful with that. I believe in helping others. The best way to grow is by helping each other to succeed. However, I DO NOT believe in helping people who do not want to help themselves or people whose intentions are only to help themselves by taking undue advantage of the help.

MY TWO CENTS ON FINANCIAL LITERACY

I'm nowhere near being rich or an expert on finances, but there might be something you can take from this section.

One of my goals in life is to not have a job and live off my investments. Since I don't come from wealth, I understand I have to work hard, and most importantly, I really need to be smart.

At twenty-four, I bought a house and have rented it for more than a year already. The house isn't only paying itself and providing me with a place to live, it's also leaving me a 300 dollar profit every month.

At twenty-five, as I'm writing this, I am now in the process of looking to buy an apartment.

Maybe those statements make me sound a little "arrogant" and "too optimistic," but let me explain something.

As we get older, money will play a huge role in our lives. As we get older, our responsibilities will grow. As we get older, we will get sick, just like we see with some of our parents and grandparents. You will need money for all that, and if you don't have it, you will be stressed and desperate. That will affect not only you but everyone around you.

It is not fair to work a whole lifetime and never amount to anything for you and your family.

It is also not fair to leave your parents' medical bills on the most financially stable offspring. Why didn't you amount what he/she amounted? (It's a rhetorical question; nobody cares about the excuse. Let's just do better.) And if you want to become a parent, make it easy on your kids to not be in a situation where you will have to depend on them for everything in the future.

What do I suggest? Well, first of all, get your fucking mind right.

I've seen some of my friends and family post memes and statuses about how money comes and goes and how we're only going to live once, so we have to spoil ourselves. And while we should spoil ourselves and not live just to work, we have to learn to have a balance (that's a double entendre if your mind is sharp) because the whole "money comes and goes" philosophy is mindless.

If you teach yourself never to deprive yourself of anything while barely having enough, it will just be a matter of time before you can't afford shit. And ironically enough, you will eventually be forced to deprive yourself of everything just to have enough.

The other thing I would suggest is investing in something that will give you money even when you can't function physically. My idea was to buy a property and hopefully be able to keep buying more. I can't guarantee it'll give me money my whole life, but at least I'm trying to figure it out, and the fact I started early gives me an advantage. In case it doesn't work out, I can try something else. I'm also always open to better ideas or conversations with people willing to introduce better methods or instruction on making more money (not from you people working pyramid schemes).

I'm not suggesting everybody do this specifically but think of something to invest in. Don't bust your ass your whole life for a company that is not yours without building something of your own. That company will not hesitate to put you on your ass when you're no longer valuable to them.

If I ever have a son or daughter, they should grasp this concept. They should take my two cents and make four using their brains, not just their body.

Kanye West said it best,

"Having money isn't everything, not having it, is."

GREED

There was a lot said in the section about sloth and financial literacy.

The main message was to work for your family, not to work for yourself. The greatest satisfaction you can get in this life is to give to those you love. I love my family, and they are the main reason why I'm ambitious. Of course, I want to have nice things for myself, which motivates me to work harder. But my priority isn't to be a millionaire or live a lavish lifestyle — it would be cool, but that's not what is most important to me at all. Family is and will always be.

Money, unfortunately, plays a big role in this world, and your kids won't be fed by hugs, kisses, or quality time. Nevertheless, the best thing you can give somebody you care about is your undivided attention.

If you can provide for your family or loved ones, money will bring you more happiness. Then comes a time when more money does not equate to more happiness. It actually equates to more unhappiness due to greed.

If you're a person who agreed with my earlier idea of providing for your family, but the cost is to never make time for them because you want to keep making more and more money, ask yourself this: What good is there sending your daughter to school with the most expensive clothes if her father/mother can't find the time to tell her she looks beautiful in them? What good is buying your kids the best equipment to play sports when you don't even know if they're good at sports or if they even like what they're playing? Yeah, you're providing your family with financial stability, but that's not good enough if your family isn't mentally stable due to your lack of presence.

As much as I understand the value of money, anybody who is greedy will always be poor in my eyes. The only thing worse than having no money in this world is to have all the money, just to have nothing else.

PRIDE

"Be careful putting your pride on a pedestal, you might just end up alone with it on this earth filled with great individuals." - Francisco Gallardo

---

The word pride can be used under different contexts, but the emotion derives from the same place: our ego.

Pride can reflect in our vanity. Vanity is excessive pride in oneself when it comes to how much we value our looks or abilities.

We should feel proud about our characteristics, but nothing is good in excess.

It is good to be confident, but being arrogant is not.

"Confidence is the food of the wise, but the liquor of the fool." (I heard this in an episode of the office, but it's still a pretty real quote)

Do not be fooled into thinking you are better than the rest, but be wise enough to believe you are special.

Pride can also reflect in our dignity. Dignity is the state or quality of being worthy of honor or respect.

It is good to have dignity because we deserve respect, not just from others but from ourselves. However, too much dignity can often make you ignorant. Thinking you deserve the highest of respect will make you look at a lot of things as disrespectful.

Often the people with the highest pride regarding dignity are the dumbest people I've ever encountered. To them, being taught anything by somebody else is equivalent to admitting that person knows something they don't. Instead of being appreciative of that person, they hold resentment towards them. They hold resentment towards that person because they find it insulting for others to assume they're not smart enough to know that already.

If you've read this far in my book, it is safe to assume you are smart enough to allow yourself to learn from someone. So, I want to finish this section by helping you understand why it is okay to always be the bigger person when it comes to disagreements with the people you love.

My sister is literally my best friend. She is fun to be around, and I could talk to her about anything. But just like with any relationship, it has its ups and downs. We both have opinionated minds, and because we can talk about anything, this can sometimes lead to arguments.

There came a time when we would get mad at each other over these arguments, and so we would stop speaking for a while until one of us decided to reach out to one another. She has never been the one to reach out to me during those times.

I can come off arrogant about things I'm passionate about, and I'm definitely not always right, but I'm also not always wrong.

During those fights, my pride (dignity) would kick in, and I would tell myself, "Don't reach out to her, fuck that! It's always me to reach out. If she doesn't reach out to me, it's clear she doesn't give a fuck about our relationship, so why should I?"

I will never stop reaching out to my sister (unless she really has no interest in associating with me, which there have never been any signs of that unless we allow pride to get in the way). That relationship is just too important to me, and I just don't lose anything being the one to reach out. My sister has done more for me than any friend of mine ever has, and to be honest, her not reaching out doesn't even have anything to do with me. She just sometimes has trouble overcoming her own pride when it comes to disagreements, and I'm glad that's not the case for me anymore.

I'm glad that's not the case for me anymore because people die unexpectedly every day. It brings me joy to know I'm not holding resentment for anybody in this world, especially for anybody I got or had a genuine love for in my life.

SIDE NOTE: I want to be clear that I'm not saying to be submissive in character to anybody or tolerate disrespect from anyone, but to recognize the bigger picture of your relationships. Holding resentment because of an argument or disagreement is often not worth losing the relationship you have with somebody you really love.

ENVY

We all feel envious at times in our lives, some more often than others. The best way to work on your envy is to work and focus on yourself. When you're comfortable with who you are, you'd feel envy towards others a lot less.

Just like you don't want to have too much vanity, you also don't want to have any self-esteem.

Most people understand envy is bad, but most people also refuse to accept they have it, which impedes them from working on it.

If you're somebody who feels like other people's success means your failure, you might be somebody who doesn't understand jealousy, or somebody who does not work on controlling their jealousy.

Using others to influence you to be a better you is good, but the real competition should always be trying to be better than who you used to be.

Competition is not to be mistaken with jealousy. It is okay for competition to influence you to be better, but you will never be better if you're jealous of the competition itself.

LUST

Having various sexual experiences helped me understand many things about lust from a male's perspective.

Men want to fuck everything, naturally. We can have the most picture-perfect woman and still desire to have sex with the next attractive woman we see.

Of course a good woman might help influence a man to make reasonable decisions more easily, like when it comes to cheating, but they can never stop our sexual desire.

As men, many of us can enjoy sex without feeling any kind of connection to the woman we are having sex with. We can even hate everything about a girl's personality and still want to sleep with her if she's a little attractive.

When some women get cheated on, they often blame themselves. They ask if they weren't good enough. If they lacked something? And the answer is usually no, you are not to blame for our shortcomings. When women usually ask themselves these things, it's because in their minds, those are the reasons why they would cheat, so they think that's why most men do it, but that's not the case. We are just not born the same biologically.

Men can have everything they want on their significant other and still cheat because our sexual desire for multiple women is just that intense. For most men, our sexual desire does not go away just because we have the ideal woman. I want to be in a monogamous relationship, but if an attractive girl walks in the room, my first instinct is a desire to have sex with her. My intellect will then stray those thoughts away for various reasons, but my INSTINCT is that I want to fuck her.

Earlier, I talked about cheating and how it's wrong, but that doesn't take away the fact that this is how a lot of us men are wired.

Understanding our lust is important because it can help us make better decisions when it comes to keeping it under control.

Just because it is our nature to want to fuck everything does not mean it is reasonable.

Sex is primal, but being able to control our instincts is part of what separates us from other animals and why we can live in a civilized society.

If we don't learn to keep our lust under control, it can become easy to make dumb decisions like having unprotected sex, leading us to have greater risks of contracting sexually transmitted diseases or face decisions we might not be ready for, like having kids.

Of course, having children is a blessing, but not all of us are ready to be looking after another life when we can't even look after ourselves.

If you are a young person barely starting to experience life, do not get caught up in the heat of the moment by making decisions you're not ready to be accountable for.

Sex without a condom feels amazing, but it's not worth it when you're not ready for the responsibilities it comes with.

Wayne said it best, "Safe sex is great sex, better wear a latex cause you don't want that late text, that "I think I'm late text."

Also, as males, we have to learn how to keep our lust in control to avoid uncomfortable situations with women and situations that can leave us in a bad predicament with the law when our intentions are not criminal.

Although it is difficult, you always have to be aware of making women feel as comfortable as possible during the heat of the moment, even when your brain feels a bit clouded due to your hormones.

When we're horny, it is very easy to misread situations and disregard how a woman might feel. We often assume women desire the same way we desire because it's similar, and we forget we aren't wired the same. A male and a female's dynamic will never be the same because we are built differently.

As a male, you might ask yourself, "Why do we have to be the ones that are always empathetic, reasonable, and too careful during the heat of the moment if we're both horny or if we're both intoxicated?" And it's because, as men, we're less likely to be in an uncomfortable situation when it pertains to sex.

Our power dynamic of the jump makes it difficult for us to be in uncomfortable situations regarding intercourse.

Most of us men are physically stronger than the woman we're having sex with, so if we don't like something, it's easier to stop them from doing it.

Most of the time, we are also the ones to approach women or persuade them to even talk to us. That means there is a greater chance you are more attracted to the woman you have approached than her being attracted to you. This might also mean you are more willing to engage in sexual activities than she might.

These things might seem insignificant once we sense a woman feels comfortable, but they still play a role. Often not acknowledging such things can leave us in uncomfortable situations we could have avoided if we had more knowledge.

When you understand yourself better, it becomes easier to be self-aware. When you're self-aware, it becomes easier to make better decisions such as empathizing with others and keeping your lust under control when needed to be.

GLUTTONY

Being unhealthy must be difficult, but you know what else is difficult? Exercising often and watching what you eat so you're healthy.

I love food, especially junk. There are times when I buy pizza and shove it down my throat as if it were the last meal of my life. It's hard to stop because I just love it so damn much, but then I feel like shit. I feel fatter than I actually look, my face feels greasy, my breath bothers me even after brushing my teeth, and my mental health goes to a bad place.

I value the way I look very much, so feeling unattractive makes me feel uncomfortable. Making a decision not to overeat unhealthy food is an everyday choice I have to make, and it's not an easy one. But it is a bit easier when I constantly tell myself how bad the aftermath makes me feel and the risks that come with it.

I drink lattes every day, and the amount of sugar they contain is too much. My mother tells me this often, and even though it's annoying, she's right. The amount of white mochas I consume is unhealthy, and people who truly care about me are not wrong to tell me that.

Gluttony is the excess of food, which is harmful to health, but starving yourself leads to being unhealthy as well. This part of the book is not to emphasize obesity, but just health in general.

We have to be healthier by maintaining a proper diet, avoiding excess food, and regularly exercising. I'm all for embracing your body type, but not for embracing an unhealthy lifestyle.

If a family or friend ate excessive unhealthy food and they were overweight and asked me how they looked, I would be honest. The same will be for somebody who was depriving themselves of enough food. If people don't want to be pointed out about these things, then we should respect that, but be honest if they ask. Lying about somebody's bad habits to make them feel better is part of enabling them.

Understandably, we're all not perfect, but would you cheer somebody with drug addiction if you really cared about them? No right. So why do it with unhealthy eating?

If we truly care about somebody, we notice when their body changes due to unhealthy behaviors, and embracing them is part of enabling them.

Looks are subjective, and we shouldn't shame peoples' body types because we don't find them attractive, but refusing to embrace unhealthy behaviors is not the same as shaming one's body type.

My mother is naturally a skinny woman, and she should embrace her body type, but at one point in her life, she was losing a lot of weight, and it was because she wasn't attempting a healthy lifestyle. My mother is beautiful to me regardless, but her not eating enough was not something to embrace, so I didn't. I often pointed out she was losing a lot of weight and that she should attempt to live a healthier lifestyle.

Enabling unhealthy behavior because you want to seem like a good, prudent person is not the move. Insulting people as a persuasion tactic isn't either.

We shouldn't try to shame somebody out of a bad habit, but we shouldn't lie to them to make them feel better temporarily either.

MANIFESTATION

There was a time when my anxiety peaked a level so high, it was driving me crazy for about a month. This feeling was messing with my head so much I felt depressed. That has to be how depression feels because I felt defeated and kept considering how being dead might be better than dealing with these emotions. I'm usually pretty good at dealing with my anxiety, but nothing that normally helps was helping around this time, so I desperately began to pray every night before going to bed.

About a month later, I took a trip to California and rode the Grey Hound (Bus) from Chicago. Throughout this bus ride, I met a guy named Miguel.

Miguel rode the bus with me up until Salt Lake City, Utah, but we didn't come across each other until the last eight hours of the way. There weren't many people on this bus, so we were all scattered throughout it, somewhat isolated from one another.

Right after passing the Rocky Mountains in Colorado, we made a stop at a gas station, and everybody got out to stretch or go for a smoke. I exchanged a few words with some people, but Miguel really stood out due to his mannerism.

As we had some small talk, he looked at me and said, "The Rocky Mountains looked beautiful, hu?"

With a half-smile on my face, I replied, "It was a nice lil view, but I couldn't really enjoy it. I thought we were going to fall off the road, if I'm being honest."

He giggled a little bit at my response and asked, "Was he driving too fast for you?"

I said, "Na," laughed, and continued by saying, "I don't mind fast, but heights give me anxiety. And that's actually why I'm taking the bus as opposed to flying."

Without any real information about myself, he responded, "You know what your problem is?"

"What?" I replied, pretending to be interested in what his response might be because, in my head, I was really thinking, "Oh yes, please tell me about my problems; person I just met two minutes ago."

In a very calm manner, he said, "You worry too much about not being in control of the future."

The moment he said that, my ears perked up because I did not expect something so accurate to come out of this stranger's mouth, and so I responded, feeling a little astonished, "Yeah, maybe I just need to think of other things."

He then continued by saying, "Think about your past for assurance and focus on your present to be able to enjoy life. You've been on a plane before and you've made it to your destination safely, and so have millions of other people. You've been on a bus before, and same thing with that, so stop focusing on the worst-case scenario that is not likely to happen."

His responses were so fucking confident and intelligent to me. I wondered if he was a psychologist, so I had to ask him, "Ey bro, what do you do for a living?"

He then again, giving off a very mellow vibe, said to me, "I'm learning this road because I want to be a bus driver."

I then responded, "That's cool, man." And before walking back inside the bus, I told him, "Hey, Ima keep in mind what you just told me, thanks bro."

The bus had two seats on each side of the aisle; I was sitting on the outer part of a pair. When Miguel came in, he sat next to me on the other outer seat of the set of pairs across the aisle.

Once we were situated, he said to me, "Ey, before you get comfortable to fall asleep, let me ask you something."

I sat up, looked at him, and said, "Sure, what's up, bro?"

"Do you believe in God?" he asked.

"I do, actually," I replied.

And the last thing he said to me was, "Maybe you should also work on strengthening your relationship with him. Only God is really in control of that future you keep worrying about."

That shit hit me like crazy because for a second, I almost replied, intending to get into a debate and proving him wrong by telling him I did have a strong relationship with God, but instead, I just replied by saying, "You know what, Ima do that bro."

Before falling asleep, I sat back and thought about my pain for a couple of minutes, and those past three years that were the hardest of my life, I stopped praying and putting faith in God. All faith was on me. Everything was my responsibility, and everything was my accomplishment.

Praying to God for help and meeting a stranger in the grey hound that said exactly what I needed to hear a month after could just be a coincidence to some, but to me, it's not.

That felt like God talking through somebody when I needed him the most after pleading for his help.

I still have anxiety, but it hasn't been as bad as it was that month, and trust me, that month really made me empathize with people who decide to take their life. If my anxiety had continued to the level it was at that month, I'm not sure I'd want to live in this world if I'm being completely honest. And I'm not saying if you're depressed and pray, you'll be okay, but I'm telling you that my faith has helped me significantly, and I feel great as I'm writing this.

"God is just a figment of imagination, but if you believe, do not forget, our most special skill as humans is our imagination." – Francisco Gallardo

My God,

Thank you for giving me the ability to write this and helping me spread the message to somebody who might be in need of these words.

Francisco's Hierarchy of happiness

GOD'S PLAN
-Purpose outside self-fulfillment

Esteem	Self-actualization
-Showcasing/having achievements and abilities	-Exploiting abilities to full potential -Empathy -Giving

Love and belonging	Physiological	Safety
Relationships: -Friends -Family -Romance	Health: -Homeostasis -Food -Water -Sleep -Exercise -Sex	Financial Stability: -Home -Income -Health insurance Safe environment: -Neighborhood Self-protection: -Ability to protect from harm

ACKNOWLEDGMENTS

This page is a thank you note acknowledging those who are important people in my life or that were important at some point.

This section is also dedicated to those who have supported me or influenced me in positive ways and to everybody who has in some way contributed to who I am or what I have accomplished.

Esta página es una nota de agradecimiento a aquellos que son importante en mi vida o que fueron en algún momento.

Esta sección también es dedicada para aquellos que me han apoyado o influenciado en maneras positivas y para todo quien de una forma u otra han contribuido a quien soy, o lo que he logrado.

I would like to acknowledge my creator first and foremost.

Brilliant Idiots: Charlamagne the God and Andrew Schulz, thank you for the discourse on your podcast, it sharpened my perspective a lot. I never realized how much I actually enjoyed reading until I picked up "SHOOK ONE anxiety playing tricks on me," written by Charlamagne the God. Reading is a tool that has helped me grow drastically as a person and another reason I wanted to write.

The Willow Room staff: Bingo, thank you for gifting me "Rich Dad Poor Dad." It really helped sharpen my perspective on financial literacy. Dan, Anthony, Butler, you guys have been amazing employers. Modesto, Luisa, Mercedes, Natalia, Nick, Alex, Pancho, Fernando my dawg, Montse, April A.k.a. China, and my dear friend Daniela, you guys are a pleasure to work with.

The Cancinos: My boy Andres! Thank you so much for helping me advertise my first edition and it looks like we might be doing business still. **Patty, Gavino, Natalia, gracias por ser buenos amigos de nuestra familia.**

The Imalas: KJ, Maddy, Aubrey, I love you guys, and I wish you a happy life; you guys can always count on our family if we can be of any support. Kris and Joan, thank you for trusting us with your kids; they are amazing and have been a blessing to our family. Joan, I am in debt to you for all you have done for me when it came to my job; thank you so much for all your help!

My Pasteur Park Fam: Lauren Polenske. Maria Martinez, I love you and I'm thankful for all the little therapy sessions we have had. Tracey Fadziejewski, thank you for putting up with my annoying ass five days a week. And a special thank you to my supervisor Carmen Moran. You have been a great leader, but most importantly, a really good individual to me, and I'm hoping to be in a position to give back as much as you have given me someday.

My youngins: Alan Godinez, German Serrano, and Miguel, thank you guys for making my job ten times easier and a really good time too. Meño, you are ahead of your time, I would know because so am I, make sure you use that for good.

My role models growing up: Coach Pepe Badillo, Coach Ben Chrischilles, and my spiritual guidance Fr. Robert Krueger. I wish you guys a blessed life, and hopefully, you continue to enlighten others like you did with me. I want to extend my gratitude to Fr. Robert Krueger, you have been not just an amazing individual to me but a really good friend as well. Thank you and I hope God continues to bless you and give you the ability to bless others like you do with me.

My childhood friends: My graphic designer Ricardo Ramirez, thank you for helping my art come to fruition, Anthony Vera, Luis Hernandez, R.I.P Luis Davalos, and the best neighbor I've had thus far, Gerardo Gonzalez aka chato my fucking dawg!

My homies from high school, best three to play cards and talk shit with: Luqman Shakeer, Quincy Jamal George, and my mf boy Rafael Navarro, real recognize real so we still riding, hopefully we keep it that way. I hope all you guys continue to excel financially so I don't have to feel bad for busting y'all ass playing spades and pitty pad.

Liz Nedza, thank you for being such a selfless individual, that is rare in society, and I'm glad to have met you.

Judith Gonzalez, thank you for your analytical point of view on my writing; it definitely made it better.

My cohost: Pam Pam Pam! Thank you for helping me cross another thing off my checklist by deciding to start a podcast with me. As somebody who enjoys talking and articulating their thoughts, that shit was therapeutic for me.

La familia de California: Tio Toño, Tia Isela muchísimas gracias por siempre ofrecernos su casa cada que vamos a California y por ser tan amables con migo, Tio Javier, Tia Juana, Tio Miguel, Tia Mary, Esmi, Lino, Jenny, Kimby, Jhonny congrats on the new family members, Melanie and Mateo, Christina congrats to you as well, Abigail Teresa is such an adorable name! And last but never least, shout out to my hype man during the writing procedure Selenne Rodriguez.

Mis padrinos: Padrino Beto, Padrino Adrián, Madrina Anita, gracias por el cariño que me han brindado. (Extiendo mis Gracias a Adriancito y Didi, por los

momentos que pasamos en nuestra infancia cuando íbamos a su vecindario, pico de pájaro)

La familia Álvarez: Luis, Daniel, Tía Lula, Tío Lupe, muchas gracias por la hospitalidad y amabilidad que nos han brindado cada vez que vamos a Querétaro.

Mi Familia de México: Tía Tere, Tío Miguel, Tío Jorge, Tío Mando, Tía Pati, Tía Chuchita, Tío Lelo, Luis, Sandy, Ceci, Marianita, Cristian, Tiana Yareni y nuestro ángel de la guarda descanse en Paz tía Nana. Muchísimas gracias a todos por todos los momentos tan bonitos que hemos pasado, los quiero muchísimo a todos.

Tia Luz Maria Mora: Gracias por mandarme mensajes positivos en Facebook Messenger, si los leo y es un gesto muy lindo de su parte.

Mi bisabuela: Trinidad López, descanse en paz abuelita, atentamente panchito.

Mis abuelos: Francisco Gallardo Lopez, Daria Gallardo, Teresa Rodriguez, Alberto Rodriguez muchas gracias por todo el cariño que me dieron de niño y que me siguen demostrando, los quiero mucho. Quiero extender mis gracias a mi Abuelo Alberto Rodriguez por hacerme sentir que era una persona especial desde niño, ya fuera con sus palabras o con sus acciones—nunca se me va a olvidar como me demostró que tan importante era nuestra relación para usted.

My little brother: I love you so much, keep in mind that you got mad time to flip anything around if you set your mind to it, and your early experiences can be used to heat up the place or burn the whole house down—be wise. Always keep in mind that our team is solid because it's built on love, not hate, and we don't live by fear; we live by faith. There is nothing we can't overcome if we set our minds to it and help one another. That goes for you too, my motherfucking best friend and my right hand forever: Ilse Gallardo, I love you with all my heart.

To all the people that have played meaningful roles in my life and have loved me for who I am at some point in their lives but are no longer part of my life, thank you as well. This book would not have been possible without you guys. I want to individually thank my ex-girlfriend, not only because you've helped me through a very rough time in my life, but because you are one of the most special individuals I've ever encountered—although it wasn't during our relationship— you are a major reason as to why I was able to turn my life around, so if you ever read this, I genuinely wish you a happy life.

Mi madre tan hermosa, Te amo con toda mi alma Silvia Gallardo.

El ultimo por nombrar, pero mi persona favorita en este mundo sin duda, mi padre Francisco Gallardo. Siempre amare a mis dos padres iguales, pero mi padre es mi superhéroe. Él es el único hombre a cuál admiro en verdad y de cual tomo su aprobación en cuenta para hacer algo. En mis ojos, mi padre es la persona más sabia que conozco y la persona que se merece el mayor del crédito por este libro.

Querido padre,

Tener a un padre tan sabio como usted es como tener todos los libros de autodesarrollo a mi disposición. Aunque no me parezca o no esté de acuerdo en cómo diga algo abecés, el tiempo me demuestra que usted tiene la razón a menos 90 % del tiempo. Gracias por todo Papa, lo amo con todo mi corazón y espero poder regresarle siquiera un poco de todo lo que le ha brindado a mí vida.

HOW TO GET THE BOOK

You can find this book on Amazon under the "book" category if you type "Enlightenments" by Francisco Gallardo.

You can also find the Spanish version of this book on Amazon under the "book" category if you type "Iluminaciones" por Francisco Gallardo.

If you'd like to contact me, message me on Instagram: fgallardo_p

REFERENCES

"Real niga what up, real niga what up, if you ain't about that murder gang then pussy niga shut up."
Artist: Meek Mill Album: Dreams and Nightmares   Song: Dreams and Nightmares

"Always going to be a bigger house somewhere but niga feel me, long as the people in that motherfucker love you dearly, always going to be a whip that's better than the one you got, always gon be some clothes fresher than the ones you rock, always gon be a bitch that's badder out there on the tours but you ain't never gon be happy until you love your.s"
Artist: J Cole   Album: 2014 Forrest Hills Drive   Song: Love yourz

"Mr. West, Mr. West, Mr. Fresh, Mr.by-his-self-he-so-impressed."
Artist: Kanye West   Album: Graduation   Song: Good morning

"So self-conscious and had no idea what they were doing in college and the major that they majored in don't make no money but they couldn't drop out because their parents would look at them funny, now tell me that ain't insecurr? I mean the concept of school seem so securr."
Artist: Kanye West   Album: College Drop out   Song: All Falls Down

"Quit playing childish games with grown man, I don't give a fuck about cars or chrome rims, I got apartments you can put your home in." Artist: Jay z

YouTube: Metal718   Title: "Rare Jay-Z freestyle- Full of subliminal shots"

"Having money isn't everything, not having it is."

Artist: Kanye West   Album: Graduation   Song: Good Life

"Safe sex is great sex, better wear a latex cause you don't want that late text, that "I think I'm late text.""

Artist: Lil Wayne   Song: Lollipop remix

"You can't heal what you never revealed."

Artist: Jay Z   Album: 4:44   Song: Kill Jay z

"I should probably copyright this I promise they ain't gonna like this"

Artist: Jay Z   Album : Major Key   Song: I Got the Key

"Brain studies have shown that withdrawals from romantic love activates the same mechanism in our brain that gets activated when addicts are withdrawing from substances like cocaine or opioids."

Person: Guy Winch   Channel: TED   Platform: YouTube

Title: "How to fix a broken heart"

"When I die I don't want you coming to my grave with flowers, I don't want you crying. Tell me now how you feel, show me you love me now"
Person: Tim Chantarangsu   Channel: Tim Chantarangsu
Platform: YouTube
Title: "KIDS ARE F*CKED UP"

https://www.apa.org/ed/precollege/topss/lessons/life-development.pdf

http://destinationhope.com/how-does-alcohol-abuse-affect-brain-chemestry/

https://languages.oup.com/google-dictionary-en/

https://dictionary.cambridge.org/us/dictionary/english/catholicism?q=Catholicism+